English Canoe Classics

TWENTY-FIVE GREAT CANOE & KAYAK TRIPS

Vol 1
NORTH

Eddie Palmer
& Nigel Wilford

First published in Great Britain 2012 by Pesda Press
Tan y Coed Canol
Ceunant
Caernarfon
Gwynedd
LL55 4RN

© Copyright 2012 Eddie Palmer & Nigel Wilford

ISBN: 978-1-906095-32-1

Maps – Bute Cartographic
Contains Ordnance Survey data © Crown copyright and database right 2012
Printed and bound in Poland. www.hussarbooks.com

Contents

Important notice – disclaimer

Canoeing and kayaking are healthy outdoor activities that carry some degree of risk. They involve adventurous travel, often away from close habitation. Guidebooks give an idea of where to access a river, where to egress, the level of difficulty and both the general and specific, in some cases, nature of the hazards to be encountered.

However, Nature being what it is, river valleys are changed by time and erosion, water levels vary considerably with rain and man-made features are again changed by man – weirs, walls and landings can be different to what is expected. Coastal sections, large lakes and estuaries are subject to wind and weather. This guidebook is no substitute for personal inspection at the time of paddling and your own risk assessment and judgement. Your decision to paddle or not, and any consequences arising from that decision, is your responsibility.

Introduction

Welcome to English Canoe Classics – North, a collection of what the authors, both experienced canoeists, think are the best of rivers, navigations and coastal trips in the North (the North of England roughly defined as being north of Birmingham). This is not a guide to all canoeing rivers but the ones we have enjoyed, whether for the water, the scenery, the interesting surroundings or nearby attractions to visit. Rivers have been paddled for longer sections, and higher up, than described here. This guide is deliberately selective, choosing sections that enable both beginner and experienced paddlers to have enjoyable trips. All of the routes can be paddled with loaded open canoes and therefore with kayaks.

The regional divisions are ours, and they seemed to make sense.

Acknowledgements

From Eddie – Thanks to all paddling friends over the years, from those colleagues who first took me on moving waters in the Midlands and then on whitewater in North Wales as a gawky teenager. They are too many to mention. Thanks also to people recently met on the recent expeditions in England. Most were very friendly and helpful. Thanks to Malcolm Cox of the Open Canoe Sailing Group for some of the detail on Morecambe Bay. Thanks to Ellie for her patience.

From Wilf – There are so many people to thank, not just for their assistance with the production of this book but for their help in general. To my wife Ruth and our children Emily and Dominic, thank you for sharing my passion for boating and adventures – your enthusiasm and tolerance is so important. For the endless encouragement and support from the rest of my family and to all of you who have paddled with me, helped explore new routes, had your photograph taken, driven to places to pick me up or looked after my family while I've been elsewhere: a most sincere thank you.

The photographs were all taken by the two of us, unless otherwise acknowledged in the captions.

Nigel Wilford and Eddie Palmer

The Authors

Eddie Palmer

Eddie bought his first kayak over 50 years ago. It was a wood and canvas one in which he set out to paddle rivers in his part of middle England and Wales. Since then, he has kayaked and canoed extensively in the UK, Ireland, western and eastern Europe, the USA and Canada and southern Africa. He is also a sailor of various types of boat, and his passion over the past few years has been for long-distance canoe-camping. After a competitive career in slalom and whitewater racing, he still paddles whitewater.

Eddie is a Board Director of the SCA and is the co-author of *Scottish Canoe Touring*, author of *Scottish Canoe Classics* and co-author of *Irish Canoe Classics* (all published by Pesda Press).

Nigel Wilford

Nigel has been involved with canoeing for most of his adult life, paddling throughout the UK, mainland Europe, Canada, USA and New Zealand. Born in northwest Leicestershire, his first canoe experience was on the gentle River Soar. Not long after, he moved to Yorkshire to attend university. The enjoyment he found while paddling the rivers of the northeast firmly established canoeing as his activity of choice. In 1991 he joined the British Canoe Union's coaching service, helping others to improve their canoeing or to become better coaches. Nigel has held various roles within the BCU including Local Coaching Organiser and English Whitewater Safety Coordinator. He is a BCU Level 5 Coach and member of Team Pyranha.

Using the Guide

To use the guide, you will need an up-to-date and appropriate Ordnance Survey map of the relevant area and the ability to use it. In addition, for any tidal area you will need up-to-date tide tables.

Each route begins with some quick reference information, relevant Ordnance Survey (OS) maps, length of the route in kilometres, vehicle shuttle distances, portages and start and finish points. This is followed by an overall description of the area, details of access points and water levels and finally a route description with distances between the main features.

TYPES OF WATER

 Canals, slow-moving rivers and small inland lakes which are placid water, and easy to cope with.

 Inland lakes, still with no current or tide, but which in high winds can produce large waves.

 Rivers where flood conditions can make paddling difficult, and requiring a higher level of skill. The grade of any rapids is denoted from 1 to 3 within the icon.

 Estuaries and sea loughs, where the direction of the tide is all-important, and usually cannot be paddled against.

 Open sea, safer coastal routes suitable for placid water touring kayaks and canoes (in calm, stable weather).

The text points out the obvious difficulties. Beginners are urged to inspect waters before they paddle, especially rapids or weirs. Sea trips should be undertaken with the greatest respect and up-to-date weather information is essential. Ireland can be a rainy place, causing rivers to swell rapidly and flood. There are also many large loughs in which the waves can increase quickly with a sudden wind. These loughs can have similar conditions to the open sea, so the keyword is respect.

PORTAGES

'Portaging', i.e. carrying your boat (taken from the French *portage*, to carry) is necessary when encountering weirs and locks. The portages mentioned in this book are hopefully of about 50 metres at most. They are much easier with a canoe trolley, especially with a heavy canoe full of camping equipment. Paying £70–100 for a good sturdy and long-lasting trolley is a very good investment, and thoroughly recommended.

RIVER GRADES

This book does not include whitewater paddling of Grade 3 or above. Rivers are graded by the international river grading system from Grade 1 to Grade 6:

GRADE 1 Easy. Occasional small rapids or riffles, waves regular and low. Most appropriate course, with deepest water, easy to see from canoe or kayak and to steer down. Obstacles e.g. pebble banks, very easy to see. Presents no problems to paddlers able to steer canoes and kayaks. Steering is needed, especially on narrow rivers.

GRADE 2 Medium. Fairly frequent rapids, usually with regular waves, easy eddies, and small whirlpools and boils. Course generally easy to recognise, but may meander around gravel banks and trees etc. Paddlers in kayaks may get wet, those in open canoes much less so.

GRADE 3 Difficult. Rapids numerous, and can be continuous. Course more difficult to see, landing to inspect may be wise. Drops may be high enough not to see water below, with high and irregular waves, broken water, eddies and whirlpools/boils. There is no water with rapids of above Grade 3 advised in this guide. Where there are Grade 3 rapids, avoiding or portaging is possible.

GRADE 4 Very difficult. Long and extended stretches of rapids with high, irregular waves, difficult broken water, strong eddies and whirlpools. Course often difficult to recognise. High falls, inspection from bank nearly always necessary.

GRADE 5 Exceedingly difficult. Long and unbroken stretches of whitewater with individual features, and routes very difficult to see. Many submerged rocks, high waterfalls, falls in steps, very difficult whirlpools and very fast eddies. Previous inspection absolutely necessary, risk of injury, swims always serious.

GRADE 6 Absolute limit of difficulty. Definite risk to life.

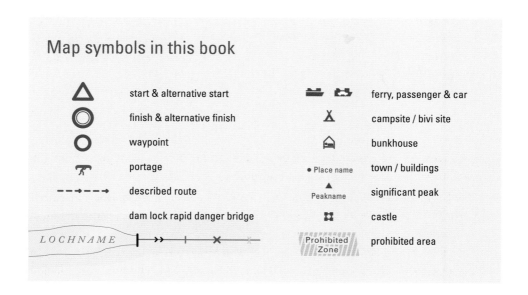

Map symbols in this book

△	start & alternative start			ferry, passenger & car
◎	finish & alternative finish	⤬	campsite / bivi site
○	waypoint	⌂	bunkhouse
🕱	portage	• Place name	town / buildings
- - ➔ - - ➔	described route	▲ Peakname	significant peak
	dam lock rapid danger bridge	♜	castle
LOCHNAME ├──➤➤──┼──✕──────		Prohibited Zone	prohibited area

Maps and satellite images found on the internet are useful resources for people unfamiliar with areas they intend to paddle in. There are various mapping programmes derived from the British OS system, and taking either a paper OS map with you or a printed page off the internet (maybe waterproofed!) is a good idea. The access and egress points for the trips included in this book have been chosen for their proximity to easy parking for vehicles. Also, the use of Google Earth means that the whole course of a river may be followed to view weirs and other dangers.

Improved facilities may develop over time, offering new opportunities for canoeists; the use of satellite images, along with other internet-based resources, can be helpful in identifying them. Up-to-date information when planning shuttles and identifying rendezvous points is most useful and, provided the information online remains current, it is well worth reviewing parking locations and shuttle routes before embarking on a long journey.

Finding instruction

Paddling either a canoe or a kayak can be a huge pleasure, and does not require great financial resources. However, merely buying a craft of some type and heading for the nearest water can quickly turn an afternoon out into an epic. Most canoeists who get into trouble have the right gear but no idea how to use it or are unaware of their surrounding environment.

It is essential that you learn not only how to paddle efficiently, but also how to organise a trip while taking into account water height and flow, tide, wind and weather. Experienced paddlers may cover 30 miles a day on some rivers, but novices will not be able to. Paddling in company (rather than by yourself) is safer.

Please seek out instruction from either a canoe club or a centre with approved coaches, or approach your National Governing body for advice on getting started (see next page for details).

Access in England

This is our personal understanding of the opinions and situation at the time of writing in 2011, and these notes are written without prejudice.

Unlike Scotland, canoeists in England and Wales do not enjoy unequivocal access arrangements to all inland waters. This means that on occasions landowners may not wish to have people journeying through their land. This book endeavours to provide information about sensible access points to rivers from public highways and includes journeys which have been free of significant access impediments for many years. However, the situation on legal access to rivers is changeable and canoeists are strongly advised to check the access situation before embarking upon a trip. The latest legal opinion (of the Rev. Douglas Caffyn PhD) is that there has never been an Act of Parliament which rescinded the original rights of access and navigation on all rivers. To date, no legal adverse opinion or court judgement is being sought to challenge this opinion.

No canoeist has ever been taken to court for 'trespassing' on a river in England or Wales, and 'trespass' is a breach of the civil rights of the owner and not a police matter. One day we hope to secure a fair and unambiguous arrangement for access to all of our waterways. Until then, canoeists must anticipate that they may be challenged about the legitimacy of their presence on our beautiful rivers.

Our best advice is for you to use the services of the volunteer Local River Advisers for Canoe England, who should be able to provide you with up-to-date information (visit http://www.canoe-england.org.uk). Canoe England is the Sports Governing Body for England for all types of kayaking and canoeing.

Environmental concerns

A large responsibility now rests with paddlers to do their best to keep our total environment clean and tidy. This not only includes not dropping litter but also, in a community-spirited way, cleaning up after other people. Be aware of the many issues associated with camping in the wild and in the prevention of the transfer of Non-Native Invasive Species (NNIS) from one river system to another.

Camping in England is only allowed with the consent of the landowner, and paddlers should always seek to use formal campsites. 'Wild camping' is probably better experienced in the wilder areas of Scotland and Ireland.

Further information

For more details on the above issues, visit the Canoe England website (www.canoe-england.org.uk).

The other home country websites: Wales (www.canoewales.com), Scotland (www.canoescotland.org) and Northern Ireland (www. canoeni.com) also contain useful advice.

Approaching Otley, River Wharfe

© Ovingham village, Tyne valley

Northumbria

This large region encompasses the counties of Northumberland, Tyne and Wear, Durham and Teesside, once the kingdom of Northumbria. There are vast tracts of open land and long rivers, especially in Northumberland, which is one of the largest counties in England and still largely unexplored by tourists.

The former industrial heartlands of Tyneside, Durham and Teesside have lost their heavy industry; former coalfields and large steelworks have long since been replaced by new and lighter industry and, in some places, wonderful habitats for wildlife. The transformation is such that otters have been seen and photographed near the Tyne Bridge, and the paddle down the Tees to a new riverbank at Stockton leads to the clean water of the Teesside artificial canoe slalom course within sight of the ICI plant at Billingham. For good reason, the delights of the upper Tyne and Tees have been celebrated by whitewater kayakers, but the main beneficiary of the recent clean-ups have been the placid water canoeists who can now enjoy many miles of good water on the lower Tyne and Tees.

Indeed, there is no apology for including three routes on the Tyne system (well-known to one of the co-authors who used to live there), but one of the great discoveries of recent paddling in the region by us was the lower Tees. The Tees winds through lovely scenery past Darlington (once the railway capital of the world), through pretty commuter villages to part of Durham University at Stockton and finishes at the new tidal limit of the Tees Barrage, which has managed to provide miles of new non-tidal water for the recreational boater. The river deserved to provide the book with two routes.

As with the other parts of England, we chose good open canoe and kayak touring rivers but this is not the limit of what regions can offer; Northumberland especially has many other rivers, maybe smaller, and many hidden gems of countryside. The Northumberland National Park is a must for visitors, where the hills rise to the Scottish Border, and Allendale to the south heralds the northern part of the spine of the Pennines. The countryside in between is formed of small river valleys, lovely woodland and a fabulous coast, all remote and lonely.

The tourist has plenty to choose from in this part of England: the major city of Newcastle-upon-Tyne, the unforgettable views within Durham City of the castle and cathedral, the River Wear and lovely Upper Teesdale. Northumbria is a region that can truly satisfy the traveller and tourist.

North Tyne valley, Wark

01 North Tyne

⊞ OS Sheets 80 & 87 | Bellingham to Chollerford | 24km

Shuttle	Chollerford back up to Bellingham via B6320, 15km, about 30 minutes.
Start	△ Bellingham Bridge NY 834 833
Finish	◎ Chollerford Bridge NY 919 705

Introduction

The great thing about the Tyne system is that water is not piped away but flows down the river for extraction at Riding Mill on the Tyne, so the summer residual level is often quite good. Special releases can also be made, as they have for the Tyne Rally held each November since the early 1990s.

The river is fairly flat between the dam near Falstone and Bellingham, but flows down an attractive wooded valley. Rapids occur more frequently after Bellingham, and at Barrasford there are quite meaty rapids (for an open canoe). There is real peace and quiet here, Wark being the only village on this stretch. Below Chollerford is the famous Warden Gorge, a stretch of Grade 3 rapids best avoided by the open boater. The stretch featured here can be done in one day, or split into two at Wark.

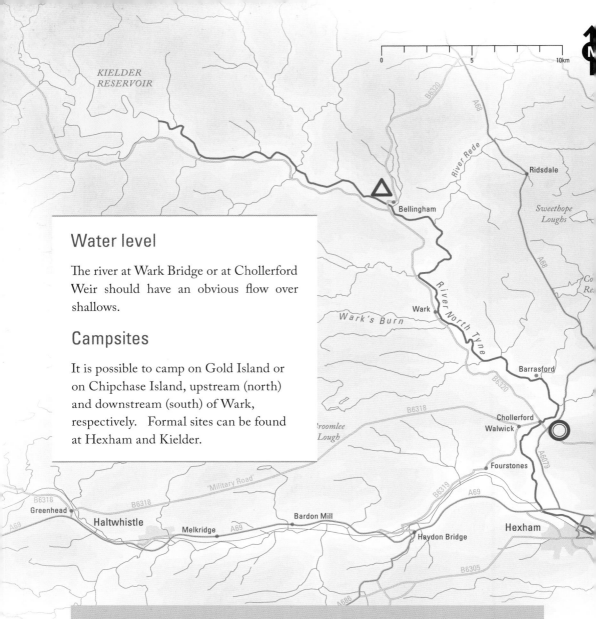

Water level

The river at Wark Bridge or at Chollerford Weir should have an obvious flow over shallows.

Campsites

It is possible to camp on Gold Island or on Chipchase Island, upstream (north) and downstream (south) of Wark, respectively.   Formal sites can be found at Hexham and Kielder.

Kielder reservoir

This is one of my all-time favourite rivers. I became acquainted with it when I moved up from the English Midlands to the northeast in 1969. It has quite an isolated and lonely feel, and flows down an interesting valley of quite differing landscapes and atmospheres. I arrived in Newcastle-upon-Tyne when the public consultation was being carried out on the building of the giant Kielder reservoir. Originally conceived to provide northeast industry with water, the reservoir instead fulfils the role of playground for Geordies and provider of relief water to Yorkshire.

Eddie

Access & egress

This is a preserved river for salmon angling, especially in September and October (ask locals for advice). There are possible access or egress points at:

Bellingham (left bank, downstream of bridge), NY 834 833

Wark (left side above bridge), NY 862 770

Barrasford (left side on access to football field), NY 920 730

Chollerford (left side below bridge), NY 919 705.

Description

Start at Bellingham at a picnic site and small car park on the downstream side of the bridge. Bellingham is the 'capital' of the North Tyne valley, with a character all of its own. After some time spent here, the visitor will forget that the major town of Hexham is only a short drive down the valley.

The river has an open aspect with small rapids for 3.5km, where the River Rede joins from the left (east). The Rede is impossible in summer, but is a good whitewater paddle in winter.

The valley then enters the beautiful Countess Park Woods with steep sides. After a sharp bend to the right, an obvious drop ahead is signalled by some pine trees on an island. This is Lee Hall Island rapids, Grade 2–3 (7km down), with a farm, several houses and a minor road high up on the right bank. Take an extreme right course, especially after the island, and follow the river right round on the right bank as it bends to the left. The rapid is rocky but is a set of flat slabs, and the small drops are easily negotiated. When this stream rejoins the rest of the river, several further rocky drops lead down to flatter water.

The next part is lovely broadleaf woodland. The widening valley indicates that you are approaching the small village of Wark (10km). Gold Island, a grassy flat area upstream of Wark on the left bank (and only just an island) has traditionally been used for camping for years. It is a few yards north of Wark on the minor road on the left bank. Located on the right (west) bank, Wark is a village of character where you can hear continuous folk music in the pubs on the first and second of January. The metal road bridge is unmistakeable and the river below here is often very shallow.

The river is unremarkable for some way below here, with the main road visible on the right (west) bank. The river suddenly bends very sharply first to the left, then back to the right. As it bends there is the slight shock of a fall right across the river (Grade 2), usually shot on the extreme-left side.

Enjoy further excitement in the fast water past leafy Chipchase Island, where an old mill on the left (east) bank provides a nice picnic spot. There is also a small island on the right; take the centre route.

Minor Grade 1 and 2 rapids provide some interest for the next 3.5km. The character of the river then changes as you approach the different rocks of the Great Whin Sill; this band of hard whinstone which crosses the north of England provides gorges and rapids across several rivers.

There are several obvious large rocks on the North Tyne where the river narrows. A Grade 2–3 rapid of a new type crosses the stream, framed by what appear to be large cubes of very squared-off rocks. These form several drops very like artificial weirs which can be canoed with no great problem; there will be a scrape in low water and some whitewater in higher water. This is the approach to Barrasford rapids (Grade 2–3) which the wary could prospect by road beforehand if wished, accessed by the minor road through Barrasford village. The foot access is downstream of Barrasford, where there is a road into a sports field and a water treatment plant. The lower and most difficult rapid is right by this track, with a view to the rapid upstream. It is very obvious that the left (east) side should be avoided! Here the river is broken by large rocks and the left-hand stream runs on to a line of rocks below it, which have trapped paddlers in the past.

While canoeing downstream, warning of this rapid is given by the presence of Houghton Castle on the right (west) bank; the actual village of Barrasford is almost hidden on the left (east) side (20km). A straightforward route is then to go centre and follow an obvious main stream of water right, around a long bend.

There is a Grade 2 drop beside the water treatment works below, and then the river slows down after some minor rapids. The B-road can be seen alongside the river on the left (east) bank (22.5km). It is now a paddle on flat water to the elegant Chollerford Bridge, and egress on the left bank just above the weir.

© Haydon Bridge weir, low water, South Tyne

02 South Tyne

OS Sheets 87 & 88 | **Haltwhistle to Hexham** | **26km**

Shuttle	12km via the A69 west up the Tyne valley, about 15 minutes.
Portages	Haltwhistle Weir.
Start	△ Haltwhistle (Bellasis Bridge) NY 700 634
Finish	◎ Tyne Green, Hexham NY 938 646

Introduction

This trip gives continuous easy water which makes it a nice whole-day trip, especially for beginners. The South Tyne has long been a favourite touring river. The river only becomes a little harder in winter high water, giving the experienced open canoeist a real roller-coaster. Above Haltwhistle, the valley is remote, wild and beautiful. This part (downstream from Alston) is used for learner whitewater racing paddlers, as it is testing but not too difficult. On the lower part, the easy rapids come one after another. The waves become larger but many shingle banks are covered, and most of the trip becomes easier. The South Tyne provides quite a relaxing river trip in midwinter, when the North Tyne is just a bit too hard in high water for a normal kayak and certainly for an open canoe.

Water level

A good place to judge is from the bridge at Warden over the South Tyne. If the rapid down to the North Tyne confluence is very dry, then the river will be almost impossible.

Campsites

There are campsites at Haltwhistle, Haydon Bridge and Hexham.

Access & egress

Although a salmon and trout river, there have been very few problems for canoeists and the river is used locally for beginners. There are possible access or egress points at:

Haltwhistle, NY 700 634

Near Beltingham (south side of river), NY 781 643

Haydon Bridge (downriver of road bridge, north side), NY 843 645

Warden, NY 910 661

North Tyne confluence (from minor road from Acomb), NY 918 660

Tyne Green, NY 938 646.

Description

The traffic rumbles round the outskirts of the village of Haltwhistle nowadays, which is a lot more peaceful due to the bypass. Another advantage is that the bridge at the start, formerly a busy minor road, is now a dead end – great for canoeists who need to park!

There is a way down to the river, which is wide, shallow and fast, on the north side of the bank. Immediately upon launching, paddle under the next Haltwhistle Bridge and then a railway bridge where a nasty weir must be portaged. The river opens out after Haltwhistle

Haydon Spa, first rapid, South Tyne

to scenery of rolling hills which rise northwards to Hadrian's Wall. To the south is high moorland: the North Pennines Area of Outstanding Beauty.

Some islands and a caravan site follow, and the village of Bardon Mill to the left (north) is reached after 9km. Access is not easy due to the railway, but can be obtained via a minor road on the right (south) side. The river meanders, providing constantly changing views, and more islands follow just before the railway crosses the river again. Soon after this, a high humpback stone bridge announces the road over to Ridley Hall and Allen Banks (a beautiful walk in the valley of the Allen). The Allen, a super whitewater river, joins from the right (south) immediately afterwards. There is yet another railway bridge on the approach to Haydon Bridge, with the village itself being reached 3km downstream of the bridge. A campsite is visible on the right (south) bank.

Haydon Bridge is at the 16km mark; journey under the former road bridge (now pedestrian) towards a weir before the newer road bridge. The weir can be portaged in low water, but should be inspected first if the river is high. There is an access spot on the left (north) bank below the road bridge, where a small road runs alongside the river.

After a long bend to the right downriver of Haydon Bridge, a small weir can be glimpsed across the river. It is shootable through the centre, and disappears in flood. The river bends left into a wooded gorge, and Haydon Spa can be seen on the right (south) bank (18km). There is an old spa well among the trees, with a new walkway constructed down from the road. Just below is a nice Grade 2 rapid, the first of its type on this trip, which provides

enjoyable waves in high water and a good location to practise breakouts in an open canoe.

The next feature downstream is Allerwash Gorge, perhaps a more dramatic name than the water suggests. Small Grade 1–2 rapids enliven the wooded valley, overlooked by some lovely houses. It is a bit difficult to leave the river here should you wish to. Fourstones village follows on the left (north) bank although it is not visible from the water. The industrial building of a paper mill is obvious further downstream on the left bank, into which the river flows. Although it only requires a steering stroke to keep off the bank, this little rapid has caught many people out. The right (south) side of the river has a shingle bank.

Warden Bridge follows (26km) after more interesting rapids and islands, with a pub located on the left (north) bank and the village some distance behind it. Immediately afterwards is the main railway line bridge and a small tricky descent down a Grade 2 rapid to the confluence with the North Tyne, the latter usually carrying more water.

The paddler is now on the Tyne proper, and the river obviously broadens out. The Hexham bypass bridge is ahead, followed by a surprisingly shallow rocky Grade 2 rapid which requires some careful navigation.

You can now relax as the Tyne meanders down to Hexham (paddle down the right-hand side of the river, leaving the islands to the left) and the very useful facility of Tyne Green (29km), where both the rowing club and canoe club are based. With parking, café and toilets all found here, this is a very convenient place to finish.

03 Tyne

OS sheets 87 & 88 | **Hexham to Prudhoe** | **23km**

Shuttle	18 km via minor road from Prudhoe/Ovingham north to A69 and then A69 all the way to the Hexham turnoff, about 20 minutes.
Portages	At Hexham weir and Riding Mill weir
Start	△ Tyne Green, Hexham NY 938 646
Finish	◎ Prudhoe Riverside Park NZ 086 635

Introduction

This trip follows on from the section before, and the Tyne itself is a lovely river right into the first urban stretches near Prudhoe. It has been cleaned up in recent years and is home to otters now. Wooded banks and easy rapids continue all the way down. Passing through the lovely sylvan countryside around Bywell, only a few kilometres from the end, it is difficult to believe that this area was once at the heart of a prime coal-mining area.

Hexham is a sizeable market town in its own right and, without doubt, the 'capital' of West Northumberland. From Hexham, visit Kielder Forest and Kielder Water to the north and the North Pennines Area of Outstanding Natural Beauty to the south. The

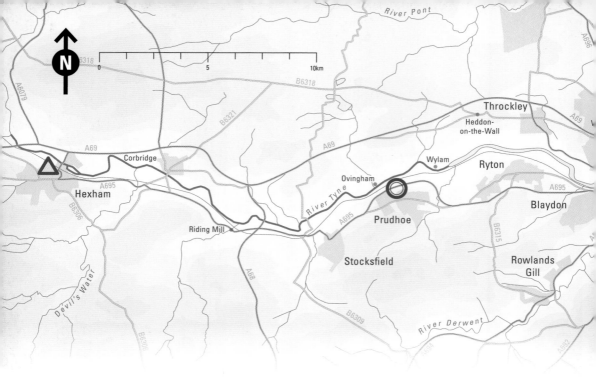

latter has the spectacular Allendale leading down to the Tyne valley as well as the long and wild Weardale on the other side of the empty moorlands high above Tynedale.

Water level

A good place to judge the water level is from the high bridge over the Tyne at Prudhoe. If the rapid is flowing across the whole river it is high; it should at least have a good flow down the centre of the river. It is however possible to canoe the Tyne during a dry summer.

Campsites

There are campsites at Hexham.

Access & egress

There are no problems on the lower Tyne. There are possible access or egress points at:

Tyne Green, NY 938 646

Corbridge Bridge (upriver, right side, car park), NY 987 641

Riding Mill (minor track from village, little parking), NZ 020 618

Bywell Bridge (downriver, north side), NZ 052 620

Prudhoe Riverside Park, NZ 086 635.

Description

This is an excellent day trip, with good facilities at both the start and finish including adequate parking for vehicles. This is a good beginners' trip since it is so near to the Tyneside conurbation, and also because there is interest all the way down and no dangers.

The trip starts at Tyne Green, the major waterside public park at Hexham where both the local canoe and rowing clubs are based. A café and toilets (open during the summer season, usually from April to September) can be found here. The adult Tyne flows down to Hexham from the confluence of the North and South Tyne with a good width and a constant level, due to the dangerous large weir just below the bridge at Hexham.

The character of the river changes below Hexham; once you have negotiated your way around the unshootable weir, the river becomes a broad meander across a plain to Corbridge. The weir can be portaged on the right side by using a flood tunnel underneath the road bridge. Climb back down to the river bank over a fence to re-enter the river just at the bottom of the weir. The channel goes left of Broomhaugh Island further downstream.

Old and attractive, Corbridge Bridge is very obvious (5.5km) with access on the right (south) bank just above the bridge from a new car park. The town, which is well worth visiting for its high-quality small shops as befits such an affluent residential area, is located on the opposite bank.

The river downstream is pretty with wooded banks. After a quiet 5km paddle, you will pass Riding Mill on your right (though barely visible through the trees). The access track is quite difficult to find from the village, and there is virtually no parking. Soon after is the major feature of Riding Mill pumping station, where the Kielder water is pumped over to the Tees when required. The weir is too steep to shoot but can be portaged on both banks, the left being easier. Take care here, as there was a canoeing fatality in 2011.

The A68 passes over on a high bridge immediately after, followed by 3km of pretty wooded scenery as far as Bywell Bridge (15km). This is another majestic and beautiful honey-coloured stone bridge, with good access from the left bank. Small rapids provide interest with a good stretch downstream of the bridge, and there is a very useful minor road all along the left (north) bank downstream to Ovingham.

When a rather rickety-looking metal girder bridge appears across the river (yes, it is a road bridge), you are at the end of the journey. Ovingham is located high up on the left bank and Prudhoe is on the right. The egress is at Prudhoe Riverside Park (23km), almost invisible from the river, with parking, toilets and a ranger station.

Becoming hooked

There is a canoe club based at Prudhoe Riverside Park, and I have some affection for this place. In the early 1990s I first seriously tried out an open canoe (it was a manufacturer's come-and-try weekend) and then bought one. That was the start: I became hooked after having paddled kayaks for over 30 years!

Eddie

It can be tempting to extend this trip, but a warning of both the mud below the tidal limit at Wylam and also of Wylam Weir should be heeded. This weir is below the road bridge at Wylam and is steep and rocky. It is very powerful in high water and there have been fatalities here. Egress down this stretch is difficult until the Countryside Park is reached near Newburn, a suburb of Newcastle-upon-Tyne.

Solo open canoes on the Middle Tees

04 Middle Tees

OS Sheets 92 & 93 | Winston to Croft | 23km (11km by egress at Piercebridge)

Shuttle	A167 into Darlington and the A67 which follows the Tees valley, 25 minutes.
Portages	One portage at Broken Scar Weir, Coniscliffe, near Darlington.
Start	△ Winston Bridge NZ 142 163
Finish	○ Croft-on-Tees NZ 289 098

Introduction

The Tees normally has the reputation of a difficult whitewater river, but we have included two sections of the river in this book because the Lower Tees offers so much to the touring paddler. The upper dale is well worth visiting, and the famous Bowes Museum is just upriver near the town of Barnard Castle. The real rapids finish at Whorlton (just upriver of the start of this route); a majestic and often pretty lowland river follows from this point.

Starting near the village of Winston at a beautiful stone bridge built in the 1700s, this trip is best suited to those who have some moving water experience. Most of the interesting whitewater can be found between Winston and Piercebridge; after that the river

Rocky Tees water

rarely gets above Grade 1. Further down the Tees, heavy industry and chemical plants make use of the power of the river and its cleansing properties. The journey described here is far upstream of the industrial area however, and this part of the Tees is a beautiful example of a wide Grade 2 river running through agricultural County Durham.

Description

Winston Bridge was designed and built by Sir Thomas Robinson of nearby Rokeby in 1763 and is a Grade II listed building. It has one arch of 111ft (34m) span, once the longest single span in England. This is a convenient place to access this section of the Tees and there is parking for several cars. Paddlers can choose to put in below the bridge along the footpath on the left (northwest) of the river or choose to tackle the river immediately with a good Grade 2 rapid by accessing the river above the bridge via the footpath on the right (southeast) of the river.

Once this initial dilemma is resolved and you are proceeding downstream, the river has several Grade 1–2 rapids. Some have large boulders to negotiate, but they are mostly very straightforward. The river flows in channels in low water, which often means passing close to trees and the outside of bends. There are a number of bridges that span the river on the way to the village of Gainford; a collapsed stanchion at one of the bridges presents little hazard, but the remains still occupy a space in the river and need to be paddled around. A wide bend with a gravel beach and park benches indicate that you are near civilisation. Vehicular access to the river is possible at Gainford, and is commonly used as a short paddle by canoe clubs introducing newcomers to

Water level

Water level is at its best when both sides of Broken Scar Weir are covered by water (above 0.80m on the Environment Agency website).

Campsites

A caravan park and campsite can be found at Winston. There are few camping possibilities downriver, but there are campsites in the upper valley.

Access & egress

No recent difficulties have been reported in this area. There are possible access or egress points at:

Winston Bridge, NZ 142 163

Gainford, NZ 167 165

Piercebridge, NZ 209 155

Broken Scar, NZ 259 137

Croft-on-Tees, NZ 289 098.

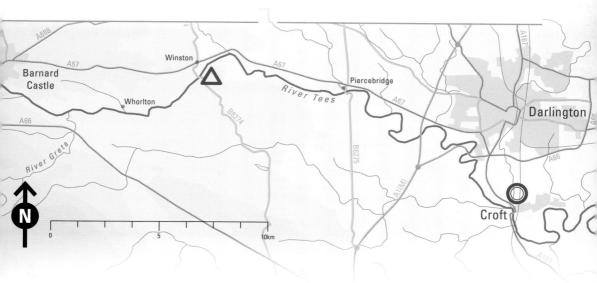

moving water skills. There is limited parking close to the river at Gainford Cemetery, but it is best to park in the village and only use the Cemetery car park to pick up kit at the end of the trip. There is a pub and a general shop in the village.

How a village gained its name

The story goes that long ago residents of two settlements, one on either side of the river, argued over ownership of a ford across the Tees. In a battle, residents of the Durham side of the river took control of the ford and their village became known as Gainford. The site of the deserted village on the Yorkshire side of the river is named Barford (Barforth), in memory of its residents' attempt to barricade the ford during the argument.

Continuing downstream, the Tees keeps up its momentum and in fact picks up a little after Gainford. Grade 2 rapids and finding routes around islands all require careful navigation. There are route-finding decisions to be made where the river is split by islands; there are no right or wrong routes, just different experiences. The first set of islands is usually best tackled by taking the left-hand channel, but this will depend on water level; anyway, finding your own route is all part of the fun! It is worth noting that the islands on this section commonly collect flood debris and create 'strainers' (branches, trees and other items that water will pass through, but boats and people don't). It is often worthwhile taking the time to land and inspect on foot, identifying the least-obstructed route before carrying on downstream.

The bridge at Piercebridge is just under halfway between Winston and Croft. The George pub is next to the river on the right (north) bank below the bridge. Access to the river is not easy, but can be gained through the grounds of the pub. A quick word with staff there and a drink at the bar will surely win sufficient grace for a place to take out or put in as required.

The Tees continues gently around bends and through islands for another 6km until it comes to the only significant weir on this stretch: you can't miss it. Broken Scar Weir at Coniscliffe should be walked around. This is most easily done on the right; although there is a footpath on the left it does not start much above the weir, making accuracy very important. There is a car park, picnic benches and play area at Broken Scar, just off the A67 on the outskirts of Darlington. Access and egress to the river is very straightforward for those not wishing to continue the final 10km to the destination of Croft-on-Tees.

After the weir at Coniscliffe, the river is meandering and gentle. It flows past flat farmlands that are often hidden from view by the almost perpetual line of trees that follows the river for much of its course. The A167 crosses the river at Croft-on-Tees and easy access to its banks can be obtained from the left (east) bank on the upstream side of the bridge. There is a footpath here, although it is frequently flooded by the Tees. Parking spaces are not plentiful, but there are spaces around the village and there are places to wait while boats and people are loaded or unloaded. Several public houses and general stores are situated in the village.

05 Lower Tees

OS Sheet 93 | Croft-on-Tees to Stockton | 52 km (2 days)

Shuttle	25km via the A66 main trunk road from the south side of the Tees, around Darlington and down the A167 back to Croft-on-Tees; a very fast 20 minutes
Portages	Possibly at the weir at Fish Locks House (2km upstream of Low Dinsdale) in either very high or very low water
Start	△ Croft-on-Tees NZ 290 099
Finish	○ Tees Barrage NZ 463 191

Introduction

This section of river offers a good two days' worth of paddling which may be broken by a stop at either Low Dinsdale or Yarm.

This is a stretch that would not have been possible to include some years ago. The building of the Tees Barrage brought with it a cleaner river, the artificial slalom course, regeneration and a totally new-looking Stockton and riverside. Even the old BCU Guide to Waterways of the British Isles advised leaving the Tees at Yarm because "the river becomes industrial and tidal". Well, it is neither now!

The Tees is popular with canoeists for its beautiful and wild upper reaches from the two great waterfalls of Upper Teesdale, the whitewater race course through Eggleston Gorge, Abbey Rapids below Barnard Castle and the quiet little towns of Middleton and Barnard Castle.

The Tees quietens down after the rocky reefs of Whorlton Falls and can be paddled avoiding rapids from Winston. However the trip described gives a good level of water for most of the year with no access problems, varying scenery and an arrival at the heart of industrial Teesside.

This part of the Tees winds through leafy commuter villages and a deep wooded valley, with absolutely no hint of the chimneys of ICI at Billingham downstream.

Water level

The second half of the river is in effect a reservoir backed up behind the Tees Barrage, so the level does not alter. The upper half can be a bit shallow in summer but can almost always be paddled. Look at the level at Croft-on-Tees above the bridge for an indication.

Campsites

There are none on the river, apart from the caravan and camping site at the Tees Barrage. There are several further back up the Tees valley however, or on the North York moors to the south.

Access & egress

There are no problems on this stretch. The river was tidal to above Low Worsall, and the free passage was not allowed to lapse when this section of the river was changed into a non-tidal stretch by the building of the Tees Barrage. There are possible access or egress points at:

Croft-on-Tees (left bank), NZ 290 099

Yarm (right side, below bridge), NZ 418 132

Stockton-on-Tees (car park on right bank, Durham University campus), NZ 450 191

Tees Barrage (left bank), NZ 463 191.

Description

The trip commences at the small village of Croft-on-Tees where there is a large grassy area above the bridge on the left bank and the river is shallow with gravel rapids. The flow is slightly better upstream where the River Skerne, Darlington's river which once held the dubious distinction of being the most polluted in northeast England, joins the Tees.

The river is characterised by very long loops in the river, providing long distances to paddle but short shuttle distances. After the east coast main line railway bridge, the Tees becomes confined within high banks. A long island follows with the main flow down the right side and, after a long bend to the left then right, you will arrive at Hurworth-on-

Tees (5.5km). This is the first of a number of very typical English country villages on this route, replete with pubs, not found very often in the rest of northeast England. A rickety footbridge plastered with 'Private' notices indicates the road alongside the river (NZ 311 010).

After another enormous bend, you arrive at Neasham (8.5km, NZ 326 102) which is located on the left bank; its flood banks are obvious. From here to the next bridge (NZ 346 114) at Low Dinsdale is a massive 15.5km by river, although the distance across the land route is only about 2km.

This is quite an isolated area with only a few farms, the hamlet of Sockburn high above the river, a footbridge and a private road bridge. At 22km is a weir at Fish Locks House. It can be shot in medium water on the extreme right at quite a gentle gradient, or portaged over in low water; it is dangerous in high water, however.

The road bridge at Low Dinsdale should be used carefully; a very narrow road near the right (east) bank is 8 slow kilometres south to the B1264, and not recommended. The bridge has literally one parking place and the approaches are very narrow. The lack of suitable access locations in this area provides an incentive to paddling the whole of this stretch without leaving a vehicle anywhere.

Middleton One Row village is located on the left (east) bank after another 2km, but again has no easy access or egress.

Another long stretch of 9km ends at Yarm, with only the village of Low Worsall on the right (south) bank providing any obvious sign of habitation. At 40km, Yarm (an attractive commuter village for Teesside) is a major stopping point with egress on the right bank between the railway bridge and main road bridge; Egglescliffe is on the left bank. The 8km to Stockton is rather drab countryside with hints of industrial remains as well as new housing estates; Stockton announces the urban area proper. Most of your surroundings here are new, with sparkling office blocks and part of Durham University on the right bank.

Within sight now is the Tees Barrage. A view of Middlesbrough lies beyond, including on a clear day that of the astonishing Transporter Bridge.

06 River Wear

OS Maps 88 | Durham to Finchale Priory | 8km

Shuttle	The drive to the finish is short (10 min) but complicated (see Access & egress).
Start	△ Car park by the river in Durham City at the downstream end of the built-up area known as 'The Sands' (NZ 274 429). Turn left (if coming uphill into Providence Row) off the main shopping street of Claypath and Gilegate, then left at the bottom of the hill towards signposted car parks.
Finish	○ Campsite at Finchale Priory, NZ 296 472

Introduction

This lovely short trip among lush woodland, yet very near to the urban areas of Durham City and Washington New Town, is a surprising paddle. The Wear is a long river with a wild upper valley. It is not paddled as much as the Tyne and Tees (although it has been paddled from at least as far upriver as Stanhope), and there is 80km of river from Wolsingham down to the sea. By the time the river reaches Bishop Auckland, it meanders among gravel workings with weirs and small rapids. Here industry has left its mark on the valley from the lead mines higher up to the coalfields in the lower half of the river, all no longer worked.

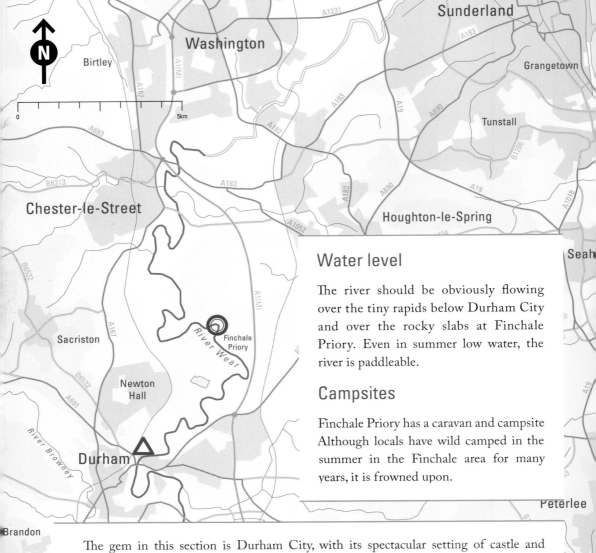

Water level

The river should be obviously flowing over the tiny rapids below Durham City and over the rocky slabs at Finchale Priory. Even in summer low water, the river is paddleable.

Campsites

Finchale Priory has a caravan and campsite Although locals have wild camped in the summer in the Finchale area for many years, it is frowned upon.

The gem in this section is Durham City, with its spectacular setting of castle and cathedral high above long bends of the river. The University is much more like Oxbridge than newer universities, with individual colleges scattered all around this small city. The city centre is worth at least a half-day wander for its individual shops, river setting and one of the most fabulous cathedrals in Europe (easily matching some of the great French cathedrals). Many people only glimpse the cathedral from a train on the east coast main line crossing the viaduct high above the city, and always intend to go back: make sure you visit it!

Durham Cathedral was built over 40 years commencing in 1093, and is regarded as a masterpiece of Norman architecture with monumental decorated arches and a length of 143m. The nave is so high that the roof seems to disappear into darkness; the experience of a sung service is quite something. The cathedral, high above the river, is only a short walk from the centre of the city.

Finchale Abbey

Access & egress

The section described is a very popular part of this river, which has been paddled continuously for many years. There are objections below this stretch, between Finchale and the tidal limit. All parking incurs a fee. The area around Durham City is a very large loop, and has been used freely for many years as a rowing course. There are no other access points on this stretch of river.

The shuttle is slightly complicated: from the centre of Durham city, take the A691 road north up a long hill, forking right at a roundabout to Aykley Heads and Framwellgate Moor. This is Newton Hall estate, and your destination lies at the end of a road which passes Low Newton Remand Centre and Frankland Prison (if lost, pedestrians will know where to send you). Keep taking right turns until you pass the two prisons. Turn left after passing Frankland, following the signs for Finchale. The narrow road winds around bends and downhill until the barrier (payment to enter) comes into sight when Finchale is reached. This should only be a 10-minute drive.

Description

There are several weirs through Durham; the last and most complicated weir consists of three drops, straightforward for kayaks but not so easy for canoes. The route commences just downstream of this weir, among high concrete flood barriers. This stretch is used by

Sunderland Canoe Club for a traditional canoe and kayak event every Boxing Day to blow away the cobwebs; a good water level is usually guaranteed (if not some ice as well).

The scenery at first is of fields and riverside trees with easy little rapids. The piers of an old railway bridge come into view after 5km. The river bends sharply to the right and then to the left 1km further on, with fast water and swirls. The river then enters a gorge, a bit of a surprise in the surrounding landscape, and broadleaf woodland crowds in. Small drops continue and another old bridge appears overhead.

The advent of the ruin of Finchale Priory (8km) is announced by slightly more difficult rocky drops and the appearance of a footbridge. This kilometre or so of fast water provides useful breakouts for practice in an open canoe. Landing is possible just before the bridge, and the fast water continues under it. Finchale is a rather magic place; the beautiful woodland setting and priory ruins are a great favourite with locals for picnics in the summer.

Optional extra

If you plan to carry on after Finchale, the river slows down and Cocken Farm Bridge follows at 10.5km. A long slow stretch finishes at Chester-le-Street at 18km, with a weir just downstream of the road bridge. Chester-le-Street has a public park, useful steps, a slipway for the rowing club and its famous County Cricket Ground on the left (west) bank. It is only another 2km to the A1(M) motorway bridge followed by two other road bridges, with sharp bends and swirling water. Lambton Castle Bridge lies a further 2km downstream where the river becomes tidal within Lambton Park. After a high road bridge (A182), egress may be taken at Fatfield Bridge.

Ulswarter in April | *Ruth Wilford*

© R.iver Eden above Lazonby

Cumbria and the Lake District

Cumbria came into being in 1974, merging the former counties of Cumberland, Westmorland and a northern and separate part of Lancashire. Westmorland in the south-east corner has an identity of its own with attractive small green hills and tiny, magical river valleys. It is also the source of the great rivers Eden and Lune. This area is famous for so much: the highest and most wide-ranging hills in England, possibly the best-known English National Park and the country's largest lakes. Then there is Wordsworth, Beatrix Potter, Arthur Ransome – the list of literary greats goes on and on and brings tourists from all over the world.

Luckily the largest of the lakes has open access, and Windermere and Ullswater have to appear in a book such as this. Coniston is a little further away from the centre of the district whereas Derwentwater, although smaller, is in the dead centre of the area. Many lake users from other parts might be a little taken aback by the number of cruisers on some lakes (especially Windermere), but this is a very major tourism centre; many families take both annual holidays and short breaks here.

The Lake District suffers from its popularity; high summer can mean no car parking and a frustrating look for a bed-and-breakfast at the end of a day. The secret is to visit in the spring or autumn and enjoy either daffodils and the bright green of new grass and leaves or beautiful autumn colours and 'mists and mellow fruitfulness'.

The new visitor might also miss out on two hidden corners: West Cumbria and the Eden Valley, the latter containing one of England's most beautiful rivers. The west has the remote valleys of Ennerdale, Wastwater and the river Esk and towns such as Maryport, Whitehaven and Workington, once industrial and now quiet. The Eden Valley boasts beautiful villages that can provide quiet accommodation, within easy reach of the rest of the Lake District. All in all, Cumbria and the Lake District provide a super holiday area.

First junior trip on Ullswater

 Calm middle section, Ullswater

07 Ullswater

OS Sheets 90 & Outdoor Leisure 5 | Glenridding to Pooley Bridge | 22km

Shuttle	The A592 runs down the west side of the lake. The 12km from Pooley Bridge to Glenridding is very busy and slow in summer, taking about 30 minutes each way. Paddlers might consider using the lake steamers to avoid the rather tedious lakeside journey. There is a regular service from Glenridding up to Howtown and Pooley Bridge and return.
Start	△ Glenridding pay & display car park, NY 389 169
Finish	○ Pooley Bridge, NY 470 244

Introduction

This is one of the loveliest of the English Lakes with great views of mountains all round; Helvellyn commands the southern horizon. To the east of the lake is a great mass of mountains between Ullswater and the A6/M6 corridor. The lake, the second-largest in Cumbria, is aligned southwest–northeast with a kink in the middle which provides three discrete sections. Ullswater has the convenience of being very near Penrith and the M6. The main road runs down the west side of the lake, and is very busy in summer. The road down the east side only runs along the lake as far as Howtown, and then disappears into the hills as a dead end. Being able to get onto the water provides the ideal escape from the crowds (although Ullswater has several keen sailing clubs, so summer weekends can be busy).

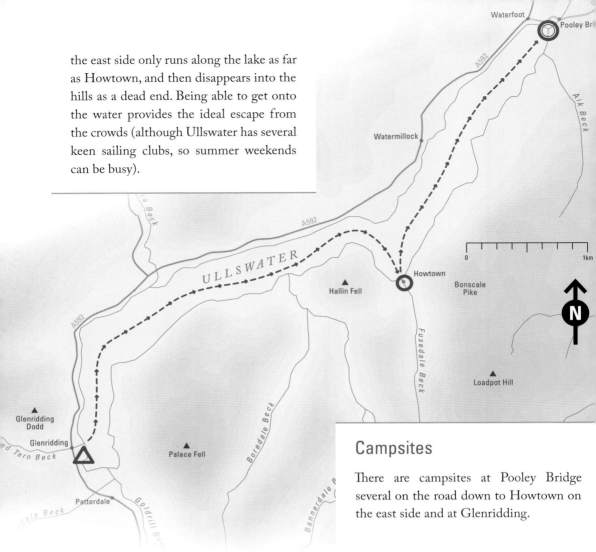

Campsites

There are campsites at Pooley Bridge several on the road down to Howtown on the east side and at Glenridding.

Water level

The lake does rise greatly after rain, sometimes flooding the margins. The only real danger is in going too far into the River Eamont at Pooley Bridge; in high water, the paddler could very quickly find themselves heading down into the Eden or even Carlisle if not for the line of buoys in place to prevent this!

Access & egress

There are various lakeside places where you might obtain access, mainly from the west side at the southern end. All of these places become very congested in the summer. There is also the car park for Aira Force waterfall halfway down the west side (NY 400 202), although the National Trust is not happy about water users parking here. The lay-bys on the road at the southern end can mean that boats have to be carried across the busy road, so be careful.

A cold winter group of paddlers, Glenridding, Ullswater

Description

The effort of paddling the whole length of the lake brings high rewards; the trip is described here from south to north. As with many lakes in the UK, going with the prevailing wind is a good idea. Be warned, however, that the wind here is very fickle. It can turn 180 degrees in no time, and draughts come down strongly through the mountain passes. Weather forecasts are a must, and if the wind is set northerly it would be better to paddle the route from north to south. If in doubt, keep to the west shore near the road.

Most of the activity at Glenridding is located around the village with its obvious spit of land, a steamer pier and a sailing club. South of Glenridding, however, there is another half kilometre of lake in the form of a quiet basin into which Goldrill Beck runs from the high fells beyond. The atmosphere here is very much of being surrounded by high mountains (relatively unusual in England); the colours, especially in autumn, are magnificent.

From the Glenridding Spit it is 1.5km up to Norfolk Island, passing Cherry Holm and Wall Holm on the way (these tiny islands are more like piles of rocks). The island environs can be busy at times, with dinghies and cruisers using them as turning marks from both the north and south ends of the lake. The east side down here is wonderfully wild, with some interesting little landing spots.

Norfolk Island heralds a change in direction of the lake towards the northeast as it widens greatly. Silver Bay is tucked in on the east side, and a 5km stretch of just under a kilometre in width then follows.

The next place of interest is Aira Force on the west side, a short walk from the lake to the road (which is always busy in the summer) and then a wooded path up to the waterfall with a café in the car park. Aira is recognised by an obvious promontory on the left (west) side, a stony beach tucked into a bay and a stone wall, alongside which is a path up to the road.

The next important feature to take note of is the defile of Sandwick Beck on the east bank, a gap which often funnels the wind nastily. Hallin Fell rises to 1,000ft and boasts spectacular views over almost the whole length of the lake. A plaque dedicated to Lord Birkett can be read (only from a boat) on Kail Pot Crag. Who is Lord Birkett, you ask? For those interested in public access in England, Lord Birkett is the saviour of Ullswater for water users. In 1962, he forced the House of Lords to put the lake into public hands instead of those of a water company wanting to turn Ullswater into a reservoir.

Skelly Nab on the west shore guards the last third of the lake, which greatly widens out at this point. Howtown appears to the east in a deep bay; care should be taken here as steamers race into this bay to berth. A good beach for canoeists is located to the right of the steamer pier. Once here, it is just a short walk round to the pub.

The east side is rather wooded after this point, hiding the now ever-present road up to Pooley Bridge. Sharrow Bay announces the narrowing of the lake to Thwaite Hill Nab before Ullswater Sailing Club. The west side here has many moorings, landing stages and boathouses.

The sailing club is a major scene of activity, especially during summer weekends, and canoeists should be wary of getting in the way of some very fast performance sailing boats and the continuous races. The paddler should choose the west shore, unless you prefer to pick a careful route through the club's many moorings while trying to avoid boats.

From this area, the west side is quiet right up to Pooley Bridge. The eastern side has more moorings and the very useful Waterside campsite. The steamer pier lies to the left (west side of the River Eamont entrance) as you approach Pooley Bridge. Egress to the car park is to the right of the river, through more cruiser moorings.

Pooley Bridge has many shops, restaurants, parking and a sweet old bridge over the infant River Eamont. There is parking and access onto the lake at the northeast corner. It might be possible to be drawn into the river which flows fast in high water, but there is a line of buoys to prevent the row boats for hire leaving for Carlisle.

08 Windermere

 OS Sheets 90 & 97, Outdoor Leisure 7 | Fell Foot to Ambleside | 17km

Shuttle	A592 and A591 on the east side of the lake, 18km (30 minutes) each way.
Start	△ Fell Foot Park (National Trust), SD 381 871
Finish	○ Ambleside, Waterhead public car park, NY 375 032

Introduction

Windermere is the largest and longest lake in the Lake District (17km long and 67m deep) and also the largest natural lake in England. Belle Isle is the largest Lake District island of some 3.8 acres. The location is a major tourist destination and very busy in the summer, meaning that finding places to get on the lake, camp or stay is somewhat of a problem.

The Victorians 'discovered' the lake when, as with so many other British destinations, the railway came to the little town of Windermere in the 19th century. Entrepreneurs enabled the branch line to drop sharply from the main west coast railway line at Oxenholme down to Kendal and two other villages before reaching Windermere. This town is not strictly on the lake but nearby Bowness is, and this is where the paddler will enter a very busy and crowded world where both national and international tourists will be photographing

© Waterside Youth Hostel, Windermere

every hill, boat and paddler in sight. Bowness itself is the home of 10,000 registered power boats! The popularity of Bowness however means that many other places on the lake (which is owned by the National Trust) are quieter, including most of the west shoreline.

The major towns and villages for hotels and restaurants are Ambleside, Windermere, Bowness and Newby Bridge. As with some other lakes, a very useful steamer service links Ambleside with Bowness and Lakeside.

Description

This is a spectacular lake with lovely wooded shores at the south end, plenty of activity in the middle sections and the Helvellyn ranges visible to the north. The start at Fell Foot (which thankfully has a very large car park) can be crowded with boats of all types. Opposite the start is the steamer pier and also the station for the steam-driven Lakeside and Haverthwaite Railway, which travels about 4.5km south down the River Leven.

The lake widens after only a short distance north. On the west shore is the YMCA's famous Lakeside outdoor centre, a major activity provider in the Lakes, and many boats and canoes will be visible. If needing to stop for any reason, please do not get in the way of other activities (as with other possible landing places).

The A592 is high on the east bank hidden in trees and the lake has occasional rocks and tiny islands which are all marked for the larger boats. Silver Holme on the left and the larger island of Burrow on the right are followed by the first headland, Grubbins Point.

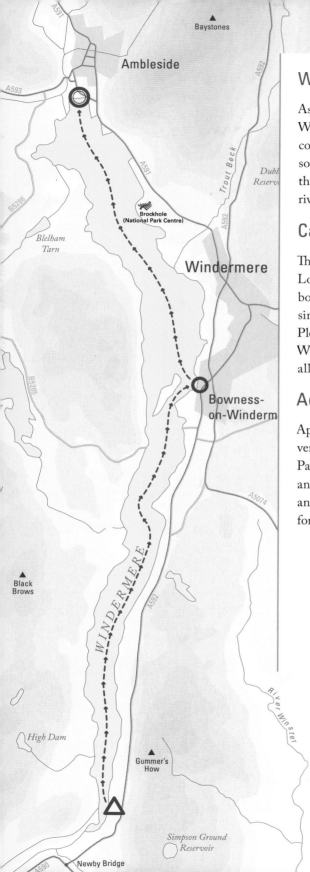

Water level

As with other river-fed lakes, when Windermere is full the southern end commences to flow from Fell Foot on the southeast side to Newby Bridge and into the River Leven, a well-known whitewater river. Be careful of paddling too far south.

Campsites

There are none on the lake apart from Low Wray (National Trust site, must be booked by phone or internet instead of simply turning up) at the northern end. Plenty of sites can be found in the area. Wild camping is probably impossible as all the land is owned and managed.

Access & egress

Apart from the start and finish, it can be very difficult to access and egress the lake. Paddlers must also avoid the steamer piers and the ferry crossing between Bowness and the west bank. Useful stopping points for a break can be:

Lakeside YMCA Centre south beach, SD 377 893

Rawlinson Nab (a peninsula away from the road), SD 385 930

Bowness, SD 401 968

Low Wray (track to campsite), NY 369 018

Low Wood Hotel (only in an emergency for access to the road), NY 385 020.

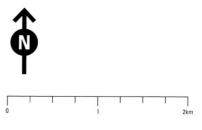

A useful landmark (often used for a break) is the very obvious point of Rawlinson Nab (6km) on the left (west) side, which appears to narrow the lake by about half its width. The island of Grass Holme lies 0.5km before it. A view of the busy central section of the lake can be had from this point. The former speed boat race course, which used to be a totally restricted area, lies on the east bank.

On leaving Rawlinson Nab, the east side is obviously more populated and built up. It is 3km to the marina at Bowness, which the canoeist will usually want to get past as quickly as possible. You need to keep your wits about you because the chain ferry over to the west side crosses at this point, and summer weekends will be very busy with large boats coming and going.

A decision has to be made about which side of Belle Isle to pass: the west side is very narrow but a bit quieter. A kilometre after the ferry is the Historic Boat Museum on the east (Bowness) bank, which is well worth seeing (it is usually possible to land and leave canoes). Interesting islands abound at this point, such as Thompson's Holme, Hen Holme, Lady Holme and Rough Holme (11km). The job of canoeists here is to keep to the edges and avoid larger boats under power, which have limited room to manoeuvre.

The lake is wider and clearer from this point onwards, which is the reason why the northern part was used for the world water speed records by the Campbells who were based further up at Low Wood. The lake bends slightly to the left side of the paddler here. After the headland of Ecclerigg Crag on the right (east) side is the Brockhole National Park Visitor Centre (14km), which unfortunately doesn't have any specific landing for boats. Opposite Brockhole is Wray Castle. The campsite (15.5km) is tucked in around a corner to the north, with access up a track. A stop may be made here although it is often crowded with anglers. Opposite here is the major water-ski centre of Low Wood; the jetties are not meant for canoes.

Waterhead is just over 1km away at the northeast end of the lake, the town of Ambleside quite obvious behind it (avoid the steamer jetty here). Visible to the left (west) of the landing site is the exit of the River Brathay, which rewards the canoeist with any energy left with a gentle paddle upstream into quieter meadows.

09 Coniston Water

 OS Maps 97 & Outdoor Leisure 6 | Coniston Water | 16km

Shuttle	None if taking the round trip. If planning to leave the lake at the southern end, use the A593 to Torver and then the A5084 towards Water Yeat (there is a lay-by on the road about 2 miles south of Torver, SD 290 913); about 4.5 miles from Coniston village or 10 minutes.
Start	△ Coniston village pier, SD 308 970, or car park at north end of Coniston Water, SD 316 977 (on minor lakeside road off the B5285 from Coniston village)
Finish	◯ Coniston village pier, SD 308 970, or car park at north end of Coniston Water SD 316 977

Introduction

Coniston is smaller than either Windermere or Ullswater, but has much charm and is quieter on the water. It is overlooked by the brooding presence of Coniston Old Man to the west, the Seathwaite Fells and Torver Common. Coniston village itself is a small and friendly place with pubs and restaurants, catering admirably for any paddlers during the summer. To the north is a very narrow and winding road over to Ambleside through

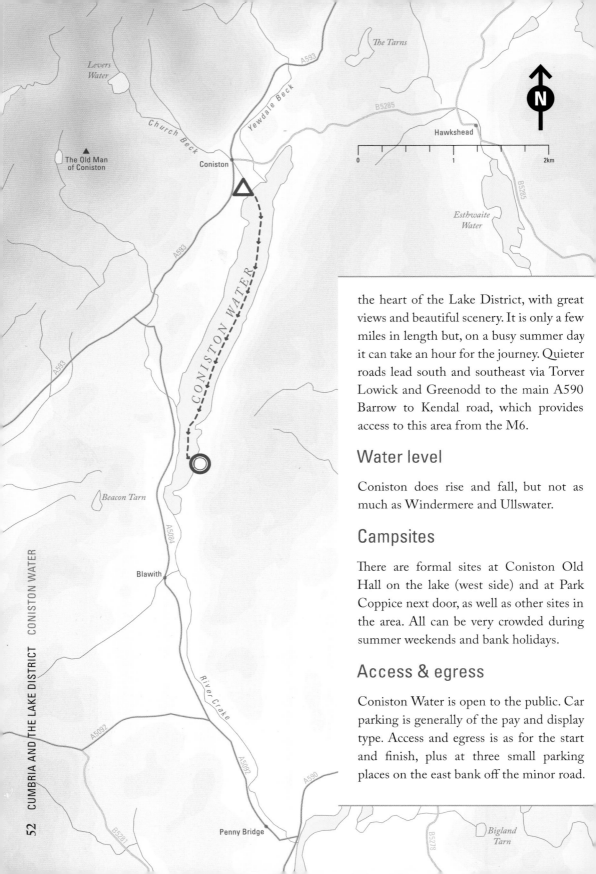

the heart of the Lake District, with great views and beautiful scenery. It is only a few miles in length but, on a busy summer day it can take an hour for the journey. Quieter roads lead south and southeast via Torver Lowick and Greenodd to the main A590 Barrow to Kendal road, which provides access to this area from the M6.

Water level

Coniston does rise and fall, but not as much as Windermere and Ullswater.

Campsites

There are formal sites at Coniston Old Hall on the lake (west side) and at Park Coppice next door, as well as other sites in the area. All can be very crowded during summer weekends and bank holidays.

Access & egress

Coniston Water is open to the public. Car parking is generally of the pay and display type. Access and egress is as for the start and finish, plus at three small parking places on the east bank off the minor road.

Coniston claims to fame

The area is well known for its connection to the *Swallows and Amazons* stories of Arthur Ransome (see description of Peel Island). There is also the very attractive presence of Brantwood House, which the famous poet, artist, critic and conservationist John Ruskin bought in 1871. The pastel-painted large house with gardens sloping down to the lakeside commands wonderful views; it is well known for its fabulous rhododendrons and azaleas which give a great display in May each year. The house is owned by the Ruskin Foundation and is full of his artefacts.

The rather macabre story of Donald Campbell's death in 1961 as he attempted to break the world water speed record on Coniston is well known. His boat Bluebird broke up while travelling at about 300 mph, and the newsreel film is still available. The boat was recovered in March 2001 and his body brought up two months later.

Description

A most civilised trip would be to leave the north end of the lake after visiting the café at the pier, paddle down to Peel Island near the south end for a picnic lunch and then call in for tea at Brantwood on the return! This is a lovely day out, and the prevailing wind (usually from a roughly southerly direction) can be avoided by hugging the west shore. There is often a strong southerly in the afternoon on a hot summer's day, perfect for blowing you back.

Coniston pier can be busy so it is important to avoid getting in the way of the Gondola, the steam yacht which plies up and down the lake and cannot manoeuvre as well as canoes. A large bay lies south of the village with many yacht moorings, followed by the Coniston Old Hall campsite with its shingle beach. Brantwood is very obvious from here, high up on the opposite shore.

Another campsite will soon appear on the right (west); the left (east) bank with its minor road is densely wooded. The interesting Fir Island close to the east bank can provide shelter if required. A long stretch of woodland follows on the west side.

Peel Island is by now appearing on the horizon, with the attraction of both landing on it and also circumnavigating. It is obvious when you are there why the island appeared in Swallows and Amazons; it has a natural rocky harbour on the south side, a 'secret' sandy beach on which to land on the east side, a lush small woodland and high rocks – great for children to explore. There are plenty of picnic spots here.

This is not the end of Coniston Water, however. An obvious rocky outcrop, home to an outdoor centre and water park, lies another 1.5km to the south. On the way down there is also a convenient picnic place and car park on the west bank. Landing for a short period at the water park should be acceptable and there is a nice beach on the south side (out of sight until you pass the outcrop). Further progress should be made carefully, however, as the River Crake commences shortly after.

The reward on the way back can be tea at Brantwood, which has a tiny harbour and jetty at the bottom of the garden. It is perfectly alright to (tidily) leave canoes and make your way up the path to enjoy the restaurant. Taking sensible shoes to walk in and leaving gear in the boats (or carrying it in a bag) would show consideration towards other guests. Taking in the fabulous views over the lake, we can appreciate why John Ruskin went to live there.

10 Derwentwater & River Derwent

 OS Maps 89 & Outdoor Leisure 4 | **Derwentwater** | **14km**

Shuttle	None if paddling the lake and returning to Keswick. If egressing on Bassenthwaite Lake, then it is only about 5 miles (10 minutes) back via the A66 to Keswick.
Start	△ Keswick Stage, where there is ample (paid) parking at the nearby theatre (200 yards away). On arrival at the slipway to the lake (NY 264 227), please ask before unloading and take care not to block other vehicles in the vicinity
Finish	◎ On River Derwent at Low Stock Bridge (farm road), NY 236 268 or, for Bassenthwaite Lake, egress at Hursthole Point car park, NY 219 276

Introduction

Derwentwater is a Cumbrian lake which is different in character to most of the other lakes in that it is smaller and hemmed in by hills. Views of several well-known mountains and the major Lakeland town of Keswick can be enjoyed from the lake. This trip provides a rare opportunity to combine a lake and a river paddle, a combination which is not that usual anywhere in the UK. The River Derwent has three sections: the Upper Derwent is very small, narrow and shallow (and parking can be very difficult); the Middle Derwent as described can be paddled; and the Lower Derwent downstream of Bassenthwaite is subject to a very restrictive access agreement. If only paddling Derwentwater, the recommended option is to launch and land at Keswick and paddle around the lake enjoying the changing views.

Derwentwater is surrounded by mountains. To the south are the Borrowdale Fells rising to Scafell Pike (England's highest peak), from which the infant Derwent flows; dominating the scenery is Skiddaw to the north and Blencathra to its east.

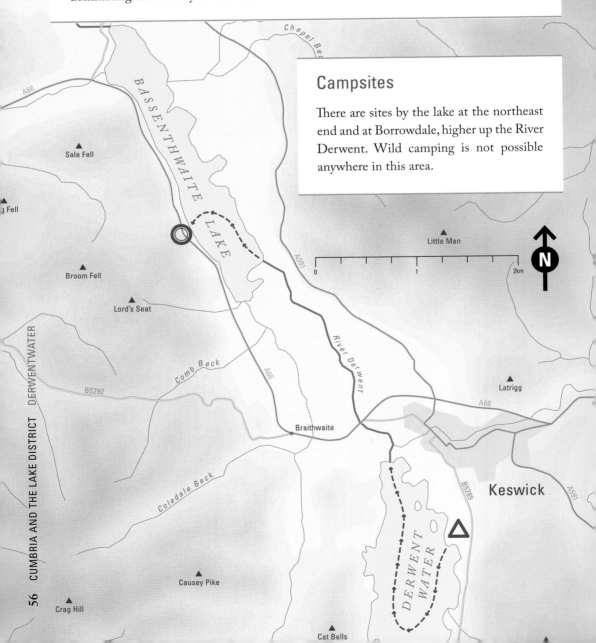

Campsites

There are sites by the lake at the northeast end and at Borrowdale, higher up the River Derwent. Wild camping is not possible anywhere in this area.

Water level

The lake does rise and fall in level, mainly showing the rocks around the islands in the centre, but not really affecting paddling. It is the River Derwent where the difference will be felt; low water can be a bit of a pain with shallow gravel rapids. The river is closed in low water during November and December to protect the salmon redds (nests), according to an Environment Agency and National Park access agreement (which should be available from tourism outlets).

Access & egress

Due to the busy traffic situation in the Lake District during summer, it is recommended that you visit parts of the lake by canoe only. Let the large car park at Keswick remove the strain of driving along very narrow lanes and not finding parking. There are other possibilities at:

Ashness Gate (east side), NY 268 204

Kettlewell (east side), NY 267 195

Nichol End marina, café (northwest side), NY 254 228

Derwentwater marina (northwest side), NY 253 231

Low Stock bridge (to A591 to the east), NY 236 268.

There is a generous access agreement in force for the Middle Derwent (and a restrictive agreement for the Lower Derwent); ask for details from either National Park or Tourism offices. Note that a permit is required to paddle on Bassenthwaite.

Description

The Derwent can be paddled from higher up as a tiny stream from Seathwaite, a slightly wider watercourse from Rosthwaite or from Grange. However, keeping to our plan of routes in the book being viable for open canoe trips, the reliable Middle Derwent has been chosen.

From Keswick, Derwentwater can be circumnavigated, a trip around Derwent Isle taken, a foraging straight line over to Nichol End for cream cakes or whatever takes the fancy. You can do all of these things in a single day (plus the river trip) as the lake is not massive. The launch site near Keswick can be found by heading for Derwentwater and following the signs for the theatre. It can be rather busy and bewildering with the passenger trips launching as on other lakes. Once underway however, peace soon descends. The lake is described in a clockwise direction.

The east side has spectacular, although not very high, rocky crags above it and is beautifully wooded. The route lies between Derwent Isle (owned by National Trust, no landing) and the shore, with Friar's Crag above and Lord's Island ahead. The latter used to be linked to the shore by a causeway. There are rocks off the south end of Derwent Isle. Calfclose

Bay with several possible landings is located just after Rampsholme Island and provides the first easy stop at 2.5km. The Barrow House YHA hostel lies high above here.

Kettlewell in the southeast corner is another 1km. A short walk from here takes the paddler to the Swiss-style Lodore Falls Hotel, the scenery being distinctively alpine.

Avoid Great Bay on the south side since it is a nature reserve for birds. There are possible landing places along the west side at High Brandelhow and Low Brandelhow and at Hawse End. The intrepid paddler will however want to head out to the centre to explore St Herbert's Island of Beatrix Potter fame (as Owl Island). This is an interesting island to have a picnic on, but camping is not allowed.

The obvious next quest will be to safely navigate (especially if there is a following wind) the gap between Derwent Isle and the Lingholm Islands to its west. The appearance of the latter changes with water level, and there are plenty of small rocks around. Some tall trees announce the presence of these islets.

Beyond the islands are the attractions of Nichol End and Derwentwater marinas. Although offering various services, the self-sufficient open canoeist might well want to give them a miss (especially on crowded summer weekends) and head for the much more isolated River Derwent.

The entrance to the river can be easily missed: it lies to the east (right) of the Derwentwater marina among reeds, and only a barely perceptible increase in flow shows the route over shallows. Bends and fast water lead you away from the lake to more peaceful surroundings.

The River Greta soon joins on the right-hand side. Portinscale suspension footbridge follows after another 0.5km and the B5289 and A66 road bridges soon come into sight. Just downstream are the remains of a former railway bridge, followed by peace and quiet for the 3.5km down to Bassenthwaite. Most of the bridges have small rapids and there are fast gravel stretches on bends. The egress at Low Stock Bridge (0.5km before Bassenthwaite) is the only bridge in the area, and the lake should now be visible on the left (west) side.

The entrance to Bassenthwaite is another quiet spot among the reeds. The scenery broadens out to show the shoulder of nearby Skiddaw and the northern fells beyond. The egress across the lake to the left (directly west) is fairly obvious. Canoeists are requested not to paddle into the south bay to avoid disturbing birds. The wooded Blackstock Point is obvious and Hursthole Point – the end of your trip – lies beyond.

11 Eden

OS Sheets 85, 90 & 91 | Appleby to Wetheral | 59km

Shuttle	32 miles via the A66 from Appleby to Penrith, the old A6 north and then the B6263 through Cumwhinton to Wetheral (50 minutes).
Grade	Generally 2; Nunnery rapids are 2–3 and Eden Lacy Falls are quite difficult for open canoes (harder than a Grade 3).
Portages	Possibly at Crackenthorpe Weir (4km); Eden Lacy Falls (33km); Armathwaite Weir (45km).
Start	△ Appleby NY 684 205
Finish	◯ Wetheral NY 468 547

Introduction

The Eden is one of the most beautiful rivers in the north of England, flowing down a lovely rich fertile valley with picturesque small villages (Appleby is the only place of size until Carlisle is reached). The valley has been less visited in the past compared to the Lake District nearby, but is located in a fantastic tourist area with the Lakes very near and the north Pennines brooding over the valley in the east. The highest point of this range of hills, Cross Fell, sits alluringly in the middle of the ridge visible from the whole of the Eden valley.

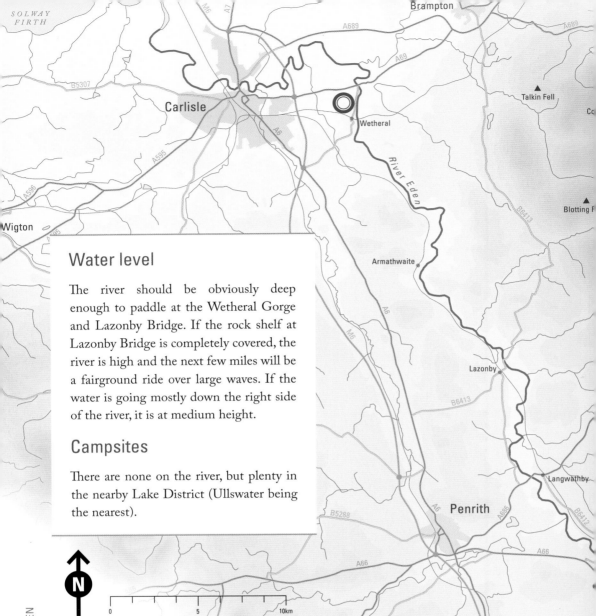

Water level

The river should be obviously deep enough to paddle at the Wetheral Gorge and Lazonby Bridge. If the rock shelf at Lazonby Bridge is completely covered, the river is high and the next few miles will be a fairground ride over large waves. If the water is going mostly down the right side of the river, it is at medium height.

Campsites

There are none on the river, but plenty in the nearby Lake District (Ullswater being the nearest).

The river has formerly been paddled from as far upstream as Kirkby Stephen or Great Musgrave, but two factors have intervened: in summer there is almost never enough water for this small part of the river (perhaps due to abstraction) and there is no vehicle parking on the narrow lanes and bridges.

The Eden is also quite unusual in that the main rapids are not encountered until the glorious Nunnery rapids, over half the distance down, and at the end in the imposing Wetheral Gorge. After Wetheral, the Eden becomes flat, winding and rather boring.

Description

The Eden is slow-flowing and quite wide at Appleby, with an easy way on to the river from the grassy bank on the right side below the bridge. Appleby is in a deep valley at this point, a quite delightful small town, and the river banks are quite high for a while The next few kilometres through agricultural countryside bring a small fall, some stepping stones and Crackenthorpe Weir.

There is a small campsite at Bolton Bridge (NY 642 235) followed by Kirby Thore on the right (east) bank, Ousen Stand Bridge and a wooded loop before Temple Sowerby. Pass under the new A66 road bridge (opened in 2008) and then the older red stone Eden Bridge (17km, NY 603 282). At this point the river is still comparatively small.

Culgaith village is high on the right (east) bank after a few more kilometres. On the left (west) is the confluence of the Eamont which drains Ullswater, and almost doubles the size of the river. A broken weir follows just around the corner and the A686 road crosses at Langwathby (26km), a few kilometres downstream.

Access & egress

There is a fairly restrictive access agreement on the most popular stretch (Lazonby to Armathwaite) which has salmon and trout angling and duck shooting in the winter; ask advice from Canoe England. It is however possible to paddle this during most months of the year. The upper river is paddled infrequently, which is possibly why there does not appear to be a history of access difficulties. Armathwaite to Wetheral (including the Wetheral Gorge) is an underestimated stretch. There are possible access or egress points at:

Appleby (downstream of bridge, left side), NY 684 205

Langwathby Bridge (left side), NY 566 335

Lazonby Bridge (left side), NY 551 404

Armathwaite Bridge (right side), NY 508 460

Wetheral (downstream of railway viaduct, left side, from road), NY 468 547.

The surprise of Eden Lacy Falls is met after another 5km, just after a railway viaduct. This natural fall across the river resembles a man-made weir at first sight. Several rivers in the UK have similar features where slow-flowing, flat valley rivers suddenly produce a fall of considerable height, much against the expected nature of the river. This fall has a disused mine on the right (east) bank, a former mill on the left (west) bank and provides a bit of a problem for loaded open canoes as the portage is not easy. Kayaks can shoot the fall just right of centre, but it is quite a rough ride with submerged rocks in the tail. Approach the fall carefully to inspect. The portage on the left bank is a bit close to an inhabited house, but is through trees on the right bank. Some fascinating caves can be spotted in the cliffs downstream on the right (east) bank, well known in the locality.

Lazonby village (36km) is next, located high on the left bank, followed by Kirkoswald to the right. The Eden Bridge is another beautiful stone affair, with a nice car park that was built for walkers and anglers (not canoeists). It is here that access problems might start, which is a pity as this next stretch of 8.5km is absolutely beautiful with luxurious wooded high banks, cliffs, caves and continuous small rapids. The rapids commence about 2km from Kirkoswald, run past the junction of the small River Croglin coming in from the right (east) side and end in a long rapid with large waves. None are too difficult for an open canoe, but need a bit of thought and preparation with regards to the route.

Armathwaite Weir (44.5km), the site of many epics, is rough on a canoe and is only suitable for kayaks with spraydecks. A portage route avoiding the next 0.5km down to the bridge has however been provided. It leaves the river on the left (west) bank and joins the road on the left. Be careful to follow the signposted route, as a former disused mill house is now inhabited.

After Armathwaite lies a beautiful section of the river which is rarely paddled. There are no further bridges across the river until Warwick Bridge on the A69, so this last 13.5km has to be done without stopping. The first obvious landmark is Holmwrangle Island after 4km (passed on the left) then Frodlle Crook soon after, a good Grade 2 rapid after a long left-hand bend. Woods then close in and the banks become steeper; follow the route on the right-hand side of Fishgarth Holm. Coat House Island is also passed on the right, and the land closes in to form an obvious gorge. A wall then runs down the river and the left channel should be taken (the right will mostly be too shallow).

Wetheral Gorge, a picturesque place of sandstone cliffs with various small rapids, provides a fitting end to a great river and is well worth paddling. The egress can be clearly seen on the left (west) bank after passing under the railway viaduct, where there is plenty of parking among trees. Don't go too far down this stretch, as there is a quite large weir before Warwick Bridge.

📷 *Bluebells, River Ribble*

The Northwest

The counties of Lancashire and Cheshire form a long narrow strip down the west side of England, with varied landscape and paddling possibilities. The coastline is characterised by shallow estuaries and sand and mudflats; it is in one of these areas that the route across part of Morecambe Bay is located. The bay is infamous for its dangers, real to those who do not read tide tables or plan their route. The trip involves heading inland and upstream into a river estuary on a flood tide, and is perfectly feasible with adequate planning and an eye to the weather. Further south, both the Lune at Lancaster and the Ribble at Preston have large shallow estuaries (one reason why the wading bird population is so healthy).

Lancashire has the spine of the Pennines to the east and some large rivers that flow into the Irish Sea. Part of the River Ribble is featured here, a surprisingly rural river considering its proximity to the industrial and urban areas of south Lancashire. The River Lune lies to the north; it is a great pity that it is not included here, but a combination of angling objections and physical access onto the river at bridges means this route is not possible. There is a formal access agreement for a short stretch of the Lune, however (contact Canoe England for details).

The Mersey joins the sea at Liverpool to the south and, south of the Wirral peninsula, the estuary of the Dee is one of the major rivers of both England and Wales. This is the only waterway in this book that suggests the possibility of commencing a trip in Wales, and the lower reaches of the Dee offer the paddler a variety of scenery.

The south Lakes possess several small pleasant towns such as Grange and Cartmel. Lancaster is also well worth visiting, as are the much larger conurbations of Manchester, Liverpool and Preston.

Low tide at Silverdale | istockphoto.com Khrizmo

12 Morecambe Bay

 OS Sheets 96 & 97 | Morecambe to Arnside | 18km

Shuttle	26km following the A5105 and A6 north from Morecambe and then the B6385 to Arnside (about 40 minutes).
Start	△ Promenade Slipway, Morecambe (permit required), SD 430 646
Finish	◯ Arnside Promenade, SD 455 787

Introduction

Morecambe Bay is one of the largest bays on the west coast, bordering Lancashire and Cumbria. This is a trip in the inner part of the bay, travelling north past Carnforth and leaving Grange-over-Sands to the west. This part is also walked regularly by groups lead by expert local guides (the walk should never be attempted by those unfamiliar with the area). The area is notorious for the death of 21 Chinese cockle-pickers in 2004, drowned because they were out on the sands in the dark in winter with an incoming tide.

Despite this tragedy, the area has a mysterious beauty with great mudflats hosting thousands of wading seabirds and views to the majestic Lakeland Fells to the north.

The trip can be very fast with the tide (between 1.5 and 2 hours), and can be assisted greatly by using a sail in the following wind. The route generally follows the tidal channel, leaving Morecambe in a northerly direction and then turning northeast into the narrowing channel.

This part of the South Lakes is not as popular as other places, but both Morecambe and Arnside are worth getting to know.

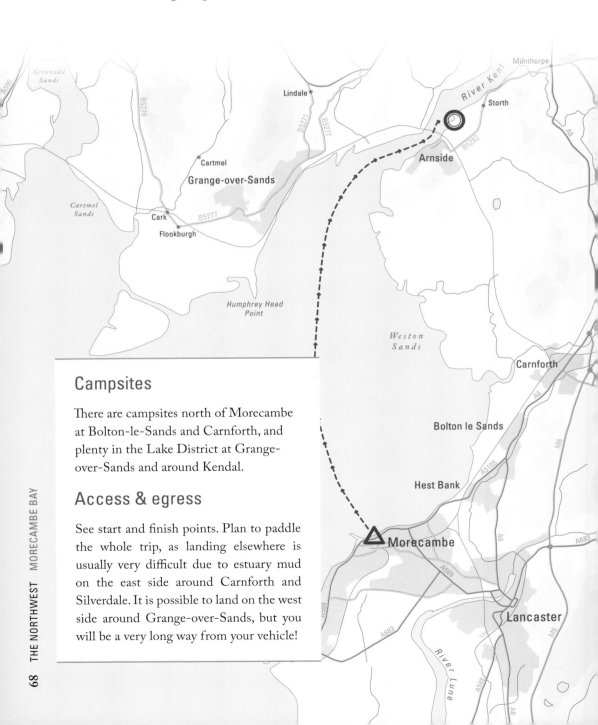

Campsites

There are campsites north of Morecambe at Bolton-le-Sands and Carnforth, and plenty in the Lake District at Grange-over-Sands and around Kendal.

Access & egress

See start and finish points. Plan to paddle the whole trip, as landing elsewhere is usually very difficult due to estuary mud on the east side around Carnforth and Silverdale. It is possible to land on the west side around Grange-over-Sands, but you will be a very long way from your vehicle!

Slipway at Morecambe

Warning

This is a sea trip across a bay which has seen fatalities. It should only be undertaken in calm weather, in a small group and on a flood tide to arrive at Arnside at high water. It is not suitable for novices, only those paddlers or sailors with some experience. There is also a tidal bore in this area which flows up the River Kent estuary; it is made higher by both a high spring tide and a following wind. Canoeing this route on a tide halfway between springs and neaps is suggested. If in any doubt about the weather forecast, please do not attempt it. At times, a paddler will be 3km from the coast. Take the OS maps or charts of the area, a compass, all safety gear and proper clothing.

Description

The start of this trip can be off-putting – the distances are not huge, but it feels like a major sea expedition. The hills of the Lake District are visible to the north, and the green hill behind Grange is always visible. The start and finish of the voyage is also a little surreal, the start being right in the centre of a busy seaside town and the finish at the busy little town of Arnside by the side of the scenic River Kent. The time of the start should be about two and half hours before high water at Morecambe.

Following the tidal channel does have a point to it, as this will avoid the waves encountered over shallow sandbanks. The first point to head for is to the right-hand side (east) of the hump of Humphrey Head, one of the main Morecambe Bay headlands. The tide should be taking the paddler in the right direction – try to avoid going too far to the east, as this side is very shallow for a great distance out from Carnforth and Silverdale.

As you approach a distance of about 1km offshore of Humphrey Head, the railway will be clearly seen. Keep on the same track until the town of Grange is obviously abeam. To the northeast, a fairly narrow channel appears between Holme Island on the left (west) bank and Blackstone Point on the right (east). Follow this channel along the wooded bank between Blackstone Point and Arnside. Arnside Knott at 159m rises on the right (east).

The Kent Viaduct (railway bridge) spans the channel ahead, where the bore (when running) can be quite violent. The town is just before that; land where appropriate on the promenade.

If you wish to lengthen the trip a bit, it is possible to paddle or drift another kilometre upriver and land on the right (east) bank before Storth. An obvious grassy track comes down onto the mud from a useful car park hidden behind the embankment.

13 Cheshire Dee

 **OS Sheet 117** | **Farndon to Chester** | **50km (2–3 days)**

Shuttle	Take the main A483 road from Chester to the south which by-passes Wrexham, and then the A539 from Ruabon directly to Overton (30km, 40 minutes). There is no direct road back alongside the Dee, which winds interminably.
Start	△ Overton Bridge, SJ 355 426
Finish	◯ Above the weir and old Roman road bridge at Chester, SJ 408 659

Introduction

To many paddlers, the Dee is the majestic whitewater river of North Wales. It has a lovely and interesting route below Llangollen however, flowing through a beautiful wooded and quite steep-sided valley. The river slows down after Bangor and winds over the Cheshire plain, but it can be a useful river to paddle if levels are low elsewhere. Finishing in the spectacular city of Chester is a treat, and well worthwhile. The Dee is backed up behind Chester Weir for miles, and small power boats can be encountered as high up as Farndon. The estuary after Chester is probably not a place to dawdle, being quite dangerous in that it is exposed to the Irish Sea. The Shropshire Union Canal joins the river on its tidal stretch below the weir, and could be used for a longer trip. The few villages down the route are pretty, but the river is fairly isolated for much of its way.

Access & egress

The lower reaches of the Dee do not appear to be contentious with anglers. There may be challenges in the first section but this is very unlikely further down, and the river can be tidal as far up as Farndon at times.

There are three separate stretches of the lower Dee which could be split as follows: Overton to Bangor is only 10km and takes less than half a day; Bangor to Farndon is 21km and slow (so Overton to Farndon is quite a long day's paddle); and Farndon to Chester is 19km (another full day). Note that Bangor to Farndon is a long stretch of some 21km without any access to roads.

There are possible access or egress points at:

Overton Bridge (about 2km west of Overton village; parking may be possible at the pub if you ask permission), SJ 355 426

Bangor-on-Dee old bridge (right-hand side, upstream of bridge), SJ 389 454

Farndon Bridge (between Holt and Farndon villages, landing on right side upstream of bridge at picnic site), SJ 412 544

Eccleston village (road to left of village, parking available), SJ 414 623

Chester, Queen's Bridge (egress on right bank to vehicle parking), SJ 408 659

Description

This trip takes the paddler from a river in a steep-sided valley across a typical floodplain to a major city above the river where the estuary commences.

At Overton Bridge the river is surprisingly small, and the spectacular weir is a kilometre upriver. If the paddler wishes to shoot this weir, one way is to drive upstream (south) from Overton Bridge via a side road towards Erbistock. Launching at the south end of the village about 2km above the weir should be possible. The weir is high and can be inspected to the right (south) from the west bank (there is a private house on the left) and shot down a salmon ladder. The scenery is wooded and pretty, and there are regular small rapids and a good current down to Bangor-on-Dee (9km). The river winds through large bends, and the racecourse up on the right (southeast) bank is invisible. After the new main road bridge, Bangor comes into view on the right-hand (east) side. This is a pretty and quiet village now that it is by-passed by a main road. Such a large racecourse next to a small village is quite bizarre, and the campsite is unfortunately a bit back from the river.

From here to Farndon is a bit of a speciality as the banks are high; an exit from the boat to scan the skyline is recommended to orientate oneself. This is a sand and gravel plain with immense scouring and many, many bends, but it is peaceful. There are over 35 double bends on this stretch. A River Clywedog (not the central Wales one, a much smaller one)

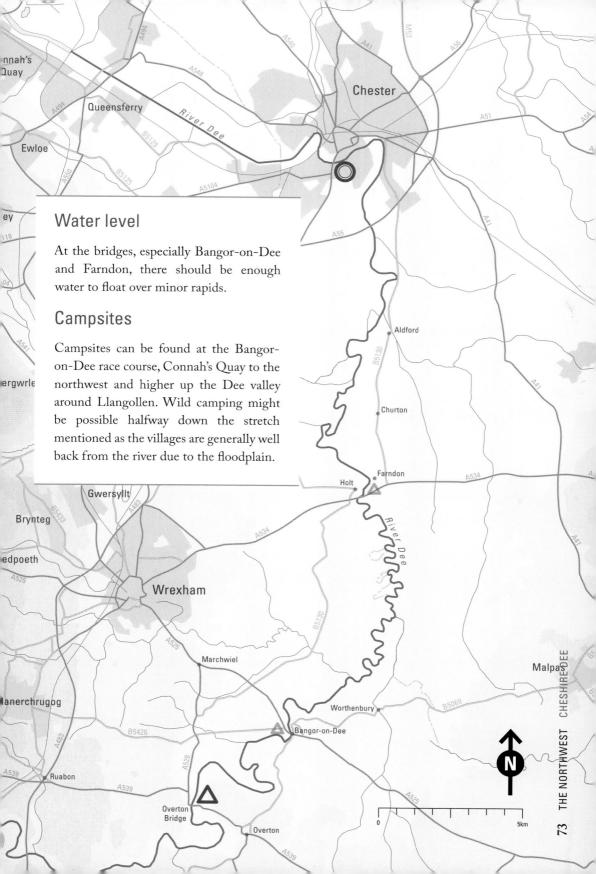

Water level

At the bridges, especially Bangor-on-Dee and Farndon, there should be enough water to float over minor rapids.

Campsites

Campsites can be found at the Bangor-on-Dee race course, Connah's Quay to the northwest and higher up the Dee valley around Llangollen. Wild camping might be possible halfway down the stretch mentioned as the villages are generally well back from the river due to the floodplain.

joins from the left after about 4km, and the English border comes from the right (east) to run down the centre of the river somewhere in the middle of this long piece of river.

Holt and Farndon (30km) arrive with the sight of firstly the new A534 main road and then the ruined Holt Castle on the left (west) bank. Both villages are attractive, and there is a very handy car park and picnic site on the right (east) bank.

As a very tight circular bend commences a few kilometres downriver, the River Alyn joins on the left and the village of Almere (with a small ferry) is on both sides for over a kilometre. The countryside starts to change with more wooded banks as the canoeist enters the Eaton Hall estate of the Duke of Westminster. Aldford village is to the right (east) and, further downstream, the Iron Bridge (40km) is a private estate bridge.

Crook of Dee is a long bend with the B5130 on the right (east) bank; the environs of Chester then begin to appear. The newish A55 road bridge taking traffic to North Wales is high above.

The entrance to Chester is a treat with low water meadows on the left bank and the city high on the right, with both the cathedral and castle visible in their marked local red sandstone. Chester is a very busy tourist town in the summer and parking will be difficult. It is best to organise this in advance, maybe by parking in the early morning. The footbridge before the weir heralds plenty of landing spots on the right bank after two rowing clubs. The weir is regularly shot by open canoes; steps down are on the extreme left bank. In low water, the weir can be inspected from a canoe on the lip at about the centre of the weir.

Take the time to enjoy a good tour of Chester and visit it properly; it is a lovely walled medieval English town with a fascinating Roman history and many interesting shops.

Upstream of Edisford Bridge

14 Lower Ribble

OS Sheets 102 & 103 | Clitheroe to Ribchester | 13km

Shuttle	B6243 through Hurst Green and a minor road to Ribchester (Ribchester Bridge is about half a mile east of the village), 20–30 minutes.
Grade	2 (some parts 2–3 in high water); Sale Wheel rapid should not be undertaken lightly in high water.
Portages	Possibly at the weir above Mitton Bridge
Start	△ Edisford Bridge, Clitheroe, SD 726 414
Finish	○ Ribchester Bridge, SD 662 356

Introduction

This is such a beautiful river that it had to be in this book; the existing issues over physical access to the river are well worth overcoming. The Ribble seems very much to be a river of central Lancashire, but much of its length (25 of its 50 miles) is in fact in Yorkshire. The river rises on Whernside and flows south between Ingleborough and Penyghent. A very difficult section around Settle is followed by meanders over the land southwest of Skipton. The river at Clitheroe then turns southwest and passes through the major city of Preston before entering the Irish Sea in a wide and muddy estuary.

Considering the proximity to many towns and industry in south Lancashire, the Ribble is amazingly rural and pretty and the section described here is the most scenic in the valley.

It is slightly puzzling that the river appears to be so little-known among paddlers; the large Manchester Canoe Club made much use of it in the 1950s and 1960s and even used the fairly modest rapid at Dinckley Ferry as a slalom course.

Water level

The river at Edisford Bridge should have water running over all of the slabs in the river and an obvious clear channel all the way down; otherwise, it will be too low to be paddled.

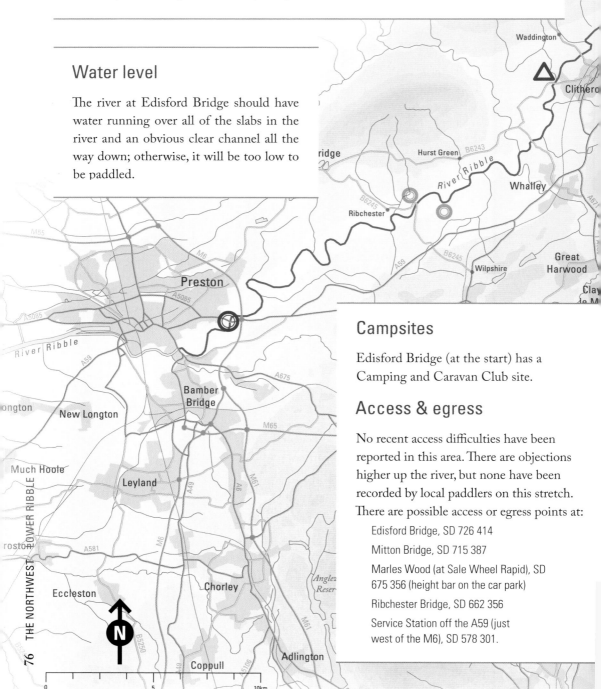

Campsites

Edisford Bridge (at the start) has a Camping and Caravan Club site.

Access & egress

No recent access difficulties have been reported in this area. There are objections higher up the river, but none have been recorded by local paddlers on this stretch. There are possible access or egress points at:

Edisford Bridge, SD 726 414

Mitton Bridge, SD 715 387

Marles Wood (at Sale Wheel Rapid), SD 675 356 (height bar on the car park)

Ribchester Bridge, SD 662 356

Service Station off the A59 (just west of the M6), SD 578 301.

Description

The first advice is to take a portage trolley for open canoes. The (pay) car park is high on the east bank at Edisford Bridge, with a picnic area down by the river. This is deliberate and now only car drivers with a key, a disability sticker and a permit can park by the river. The trip down is about 250m, and no bother. This is a really nice place to start from, with many people in the river on a sunny summer's day. There are picnic benches and toilets. The river is in a valley with wooded sides for most of the way down. There are easy riffles all the way down and several places with strange rock reefs at right angles to the river, causing small drops. The first few kilometres loop around the outskirts of Clitheroe, with a water treatment works on the left (east) bank.

The first major event is a weir at about 2km with a chute in the middle and portages possible on both sides. After a bend and some open land is Great Mitton Bridge, a fine stone affair with pubs both sides (the left-hand pub is closer to the river). Many of the drops mentioned above are located downstream of this bridge; although they result in ledges across the river there is always a way through.

The River Hodder joins from the right (northwest) shortly afterwards, followed by the River Calder from the left (southeast) side. Both obviously add water, but in summer these are very minor shallow rivers.

Shallow rapids continue between wooded countryside. A pipe or aqueduct bridge heralds a long bend to the left and a turn to the right, when Dinckley footbridge (a rather fine metal suspension bridge) will be glimpsed. Dinckley on the left (southeast) bank was formerly joined to Hurst Green on the right bank by a ferry in bygone days. Apart from being the only river crossing for miles, it also enabled local Catholics to attend Mass at Stonyhurst College, the (now closed) seminary which lies up the hill from Hurst Green village. Hurst Green is also a pretty village with pubs, but quite a walk up Lambing Clough Lane from the river. It is quite difficult to imagine the former slalom competition site now, as there are no camping facilities and the width of the river would have meant a very long wire stretch across the river to hang the slalom poles.

The rapids below Dinckley warn the paddler of the imminent presence of Sale Wheel. This is a most fantastic place, and the rock formations and sandy beaches remind both authors of North American locations. At the first bend to the right, the river drops to the right and the view is then of a much-narrowed river and an obvious sharp bend downstream to the right. There are two ledges and the Ribble then falls through a gap between rocks, the channel being right of centre. Due to the constriction, this creates very large waves in high water and it is a heavy rapid. Open boaters should be prepared to get wet! There is a possible get-out just at the end of the rapid on the left side at a beach between the rocks, but this probably requires a swift turn to accomplish. The name of this rapid is taken from the very large eddy on river-left at the bottom ('The Wheel'); the river then turns sharply to the right and quietens down.

© The Sale Wheel Rapid

There is access up a footpath (300m) to the Marles Wood car park. This has plenty of room, but unfortunately a 2m height barrier at the entrance. Quick action might enable a vehicle to be driven out of the barrier and a boat put on the top. Take care with any manoeuvre however, as there is little space on the road outside and driving under the barrier with a boat or uprights on the roof might result in unwanted modifications.

It is now only about 1.5km down to Ribchester Bridge. Parking here is also difficult, as unfortunately a former large pub and car park is being demolished (2011) for new housing. The two best options now are either on the road to Ribchester on the right (west) bank after the white line near the bridge (maybe one vehicle) or in a lay-by which can take a minibus and trailer up the Hurst Green road (250m walk). Either way, there is very little space to even stop and load boats.

If interested in the paddle to Preston, this is a further 17km and the scenery is a bit dull. A possible egress is at the new service station at the junction of the A59 and M6. There is a car park here (free for first hour, barrier tickets exchanged in the service station shop for a ticket for exit). There are no spaces for trailers or long vehicles however. A path runs up from the river to a gate in the fence, built for anglers. The whole trip is a cracking day out!

© *Steps down to Sale Wheel, River Ribble*

Myton Bridge, a nice place to start a journey to the Ouse

Yorkshire Dales

This is a very large part of England, offering a multitude of paddling possibilities. The routes lie very much in either the Dales or over the Vale of York, and avoid both the whitewater upper reaches of many beautiful valleys and the major industrial centres. Between them are rivers with plenty of character, stunning scenery and many other places of interest on the tourist trail. Flowing east from the Pennines, the valleys of the Swale, Nidd, Ure and Wharfe gather near the city of York to form the Ouse, which in turn gathers in the Trent, Aire and Don to form the mighty Humber.

In this section are trips on the Swale, Ure and Wharfe, one on the Ouse and a section of one of the most spectacular canals, the Leeds and Liverpool. All of the routes are geographically close to each other, but some of the roads across the moors joining the dales can be steep and narrow.

If holidaying in the area, the upper dales are well worth visiting for their pretty, small villages and waterfalls. High summer will however mean heavy traffic and, as with so many other parts of England, a trip in spring or autumn might be a better idea. All the dales have fantastic (and often easy) walking opportunities and a varied holiday can be planned.

The dales are all of different characters. Tight and narrow Swaledale is well known for its tiny walled fields and many stone barns, very tight and narrow roads and succession of interesting falls on the river. Wensleydale (the valley of the Ure) is much longer and broader, but with a succession of great waterfalls. In the past (when access was somewhat easier), the river was known as a whitewater classic 'to rival the Teifi or Dee'. Luckily, the Ure has long stretches of water of all grades to suit all paddlers. The Nidd, not included as a route, is a much shorter, smaller and narrower river, although again in an attractive valley headed by the village of Pateley Bridge. Reservoirs carry off much of its headwaters. Wharfedale is perhaps the longest and broadest, the Wharfe arguably carrying more water than the previously mentioned rivers. This route journeys through gems of villages such as Kettlewell and Grassington, many rapids such as the famous Appletreewick and the gorge of 'The Strid' just above our start point.

We have not yet mentioned the historic and architectural charms of Yorkshire: Richmond with its castle, the cathedral towns of Ripon and York, abbeys such as Bolton and the major centres of Leeds and Bradford. A veritable cornucopia of delights awaits the visitor to the Yorkshire Dales.

The Swale below Morton

15 River Swale

 **OS Sheet 92 & 99 | Catterick to Morton-on-Swale | 26–62km**

Shuttle	A684 west to Morton-on-Swale, then north on the A1 (14km or 15 minutes).
Portages	None on main sections. If paddling the whole stretch between Richmond and Catterick, the Grade 2–3 Easby rapids might require a portage; just before Topcliffe a weir will also probably require portaging.
Start	△ Catterick, SE 227 993 or Richmond Bridge, NZ 175 009
Finish	○ Morton-on-Swale, SE 318 917

Introduction

The main trip recommended in this section is a lovely easy day's paddling in pastoral lowland countryside where the River Swale enters the flat Vale of York. The Swale is a gem among Yorkshire rivers. Higher up it is a beautiful hill river with continuous rapids; unfortunately these rise and fall very quickly, making it difficult to paddle unless in a small kayak. The whole of Swaledale is a must-visit if journeying here for this trip. The dale is famous for its tiny stone-built villages, small walled fields and various natural and man-made attractions.

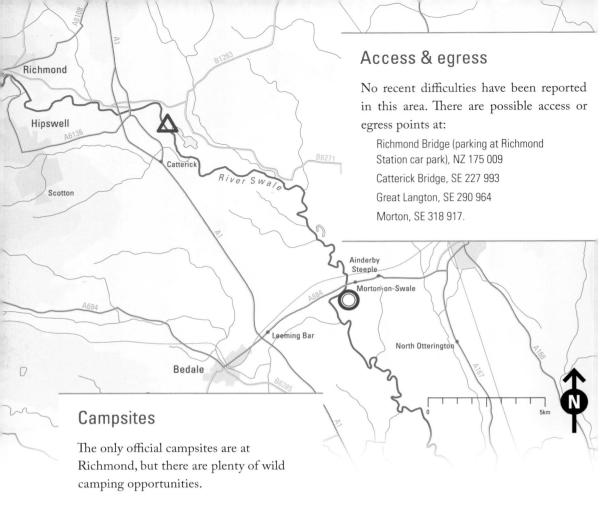

Access & egress

No recent difficulties have been reported in this area. There are possible access or egress points at:

Richmond Bridge (parking at Richmond Station car park), NZ 175 009

Catterick Bridge, SE 227 993

Great Langton, SE 290 964

Morton, SE 318 917.

Campsites

The only official campsites are at Richmond, but there are plenty of wild camping opportunities.

Keld Gorge has many waterfalls high up the valley, and the river twists and turns through lovely wooded banks between the villages of Reeth, Muker, Grinton and Marske. In the past, a charity paddle in the autumn brought out many open canoeists for either a bit of a challenge (if water high) or a bit of a walk (if water low).

The main trip described is simple to execute, has no portages and water levels make it one that can be paddled at any time of year. The longer trip described commences further upriver at Richmond, a fortified hill town which is home to the largest army base in England (Catterick Garrison). Richmond is a good centre for holidaying in this part of Yorkshire with its lovely old stone buildings and many facilities. It is also the place where the last high fall on the river occurs, just above its road bridge.

Further down the valley, the river is often remote from roads and villages (probably due to the flood threats in the Vale of York) and bridges and access points are not frequent. The whole stretch from Richmond to Topcliffe can provide a 3-day trip; it is not the water which is committing but the distances, with no easy egress from the river.

Water level

The locals delight in telling you that this is the fastest-rising river in England; the Richmond to Morton section, containing small rapids, is best done after rain and not during a long dry summer. After Morton, the meandering gravel sections are left behind and the Swale is contained in a narrow channel often between high banks. It is only recommended to paddle below Morton during medium–low levels, as high flood can be quite dangerous and over-committing. As well as tree branches, there are narrow bridge arches in places. Take a look over any of the bridges to assess the level.

Description

If starting from Richmond, the Swale winds through a steep valley. Easby Abbey is located on the left (east) bank after about 1km, followed by a nice set of rapids which can become Grade 3 when the river is at a good level. A bridge that used to support the old railway line comes into view, and identifies the end of the Abbey rapid. If this section is too shallow to paddle, then think carefully about continuing on downstream as there are several other Grade 2 rapids between here and Catterick Bridge and some of them are quite long. Brompton-on-Swale heralds the slowing down of the river somewhat. Catterick village and bridge follow at 9km, the famous horse-racing track located close to the river on the right (southeast) bank.

Access at Catterick is by the Catterick Bridge Hotel, opposite the racecourse. This bridge is the 'old' A1 bridge, and is not to be confused with the new A1 bypass bridge. On the downstream side of the bridge, river left, is a footpath that leads to the river and a sandy beach. Access to the path is through a gap in the wall which is too narrow for boats, but it is easy to lift boats over this low wall.

The Swale then commences its great bends as it twists and turns over the plain, with quite a few gravel workings. There are a number of simple rapids to negotiate in this stretch, but nothing that should cause even the most heavily laden boat any significant difficulties. At Great Langton (16km) there is a bridge over a minor road. While this could be used to meet up with friends, replenish sticks or as an emergency egress, getting large boats on or off the river here is quite challenging due to the dense riverside foliage. The next available egress is Morton-on-Swale, located at 26km. The journey from Great Langton to Morton-on-Swale is most tranquil with little to concern paddlers. The river flows steadily and there is no requirement for any athletic manoeuvres.

There is a large car park on the right (west) bank at Morton on the downstream side of the bridge. The river is approached via a footpath on the upstream side and boats have to be carried over a stile. The village is nearby and has useful shops. The river is wide (about 20m) and the banks steep. Birds and any mammals are quite hidden down here, so wildlife-spotting opportunities should be good (bird life especially). There is a good flow which takes any difficulty from the journey, even in summer low water.

Below Morton

The only real landmark on this stretch is a disused railway bridge about halfway, with Maunby village on the left (east). The river twists and turns, making progress difficult to judge. Any determination of whereabouts (without a GPS) has to be made by climbing the banks. The scenery varies from grassy banks to thick foliage.

The river rarely becomes more than Grade 1 but there are tree-lined bends that can be tricky in high water. Floods have piled debris and driftwood into great rafts in some locations, making dangerous obstructions. These are easily avoided in low water, but great care should be exercised in flood.

The bridge at Skipton (54km from Richmond, 26km from Morton) is around a left-hand bend and will be advertised by the traffic noise (absent for the rest of the trip). Egress at Skipton is downstream of the road bridge onto a public footpath. Access for vehicles is not great here, as it will involve a carry over a stile and along the road for a bit. If leaving vehicles for any length of time, this is best done at a large grass verge on the A61 as it leaves the village towards Thirsk (northeast).

Topcliffe is a further 8km, involving either portaging Topcliffe Mill Weir or leaving the river here. From Richmond to Topcliffe is 62km.

16 River Ure

OS Sheet 99 | Mickley to Ripon | 16km

Shuttle	A6108 towards West Tanfield, then turn left onto a minor road after North Stainley to Mickley (10km or 15 minutes).
Grade	2 with one short section of 3 at Sleningford Mill (easily portaged).
Portages	Sleningford Weir
Start	△ Mickley, SE 251 768 or Hack Falls, SE 231 775
Finish	◎ Ripon, SE 317 720

Introduction

Wensleydale is a very rare place indeed. Nearly all Yorkshire Dales are named after the water that flows through them; not so in this case, as the dale is named after the village of Wensley. The River Ure is the significant water that flows through Wensleydale and past pretty villages and historic towns such as Middleham, Masham (pronounced Massam) and Ripon. The Ure has some spectacular falls at Aysgarth (well above the section described) and there are many picturesque walks along the side of the river to be enjoyed, with frequent tea shops available to keep you going. The river starts well up past Hawes, a popular Sunday destination for ramblers and motorcycle enthusiasts.

Several stretches of river between Hawes and Aysgarth are used by local Outdoor Education Centres for courses, and the section below Aysgarth Falls to Wensley is sometimes paddled by kayakers (but is not well suited to open canoeists). The journey from Mickley to Sleningford Mill is well established; it has long been used for introducing beginners to whitewater paddling and makes a very gentle whitewater canoe trip at medium levels. Land has recently (2010) been purchased by the Yorkshire region of Canoe England, providing access to the river at Ripon and making the possibility of continuing downstream to here or beyond where the river is navigable a reality. It is possible to put on slightly higher up at Hack Falls (Grade 3), but it is a long and awkward portage if you get there and decide not to paddle. The walk in is also quite lengthy.

Water level

The Ure holds its water well, and a trip is possible even in low water conditions. In very low water, the shortened trip from Sleningford Mill to Ripon is advised.

Campsites

Sleningford Mill Camping and Caravan Site (off the A6108 near West Tanfield).

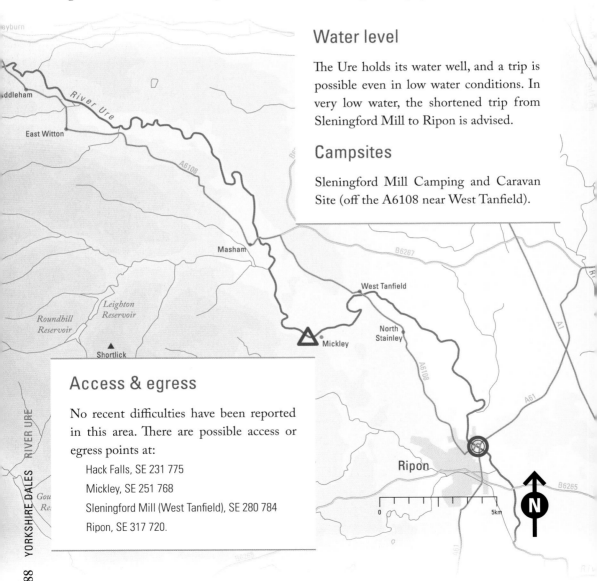

Access & egress

No recent difficulties have been reported in this area. There are possible access or egress points at:

Hack Falls, SE 231 775

Mickley, SE 251 768

Sleningford Mill (West Tanfield), SE 280 784

Ripon, SE 317 720.

Description

As you drive up and away from the village of Mickley, the road flattens for a few metres and space for parking three or four cars is obvious on the right: this is the put-in for Mickley. A short walk through woods brings you to a steep track leading down to the river. Here the river is wide and placid, but a glance downstream will confirm that a long weir is stilling the waters. The weir is often paddled on river left, but inspect from the left bank if you are uncertain; walking around is easy enough if you choose to. Directly opposite the weir, the river flows around a large island. The most commonly paddled route is between the island and the weir. Large eddies on either side of the river at the bottom of the island provide excellent venues for learning or refining moving water techniques.

A broken weir causes a small wave a couple of hundred metres below the island, and you should stay in the middle of the river to avoid any remaining debris. There are no more man-made obstacles until the very obvious (and dangerous) weir at Sleningford Mill. The journey between Mickley and Sleningford is steady with no surprises, never getting above Grade 2. Wide bends and gentle rapids can all be negotiated with ease, although interesting routes can be sought for the more adventurous. The river does occasionally split but the route is usually obvious and ample time is available for decision making in all but the wildest of conditions.

Rather grand buildings appear on the left (north) bank as you approach the village of West Tanfield, where two very fine public houses exist. Masham, only a few miles from here, is the home of both the Theakstones and Black Sheep breweries (the Black Sheep brewery getting its name from the member of the Theakstone family that established it). As the possible start or end point of Sleningford Mill is less than half a mile from here, these fine public houses are often frequented by canoeists (who have always received a warm welcome).

Passing under the bridge at West Tanfield, it is time to think about the weir at Sleningford. While it is frequently shot on river right, it can cause problems for those less practised at whitewater skills. If you are at all uncertain, portage via the right bank before getting back on at a place of your choosing. Grade 2 water follows the weir down to Sleningford Mill where a Grade 3 drop awaits those who miss the get-out by the concrete breakwater on the right (east). The fall, which is towards the end of 100m of good Grade 2 water, is paddleable; a large rock directly after the fall has a nasty habit of getting in the way of canoes, however. Portage is very easy via the right bank. There is a canoe shop at the campsite where the proprietors are well known for their friendliness and willingness to help. If you are unsure about paddling the rapids at Sleningford Mill, a chat with the people in the shop might be of benefit.

After the main event at Sleningford, the river has many short sections of Grade 2 all the way down to Ripon (only the last kilometre or so can be described as 'pedestrian'). The road bridge that signals the end of the section also provides a final injection of sport as its pillars often direct the water into a series of jets and eddies, entertaining those with any energy left. Egress downstream of the bridge on the right (west) bank and go through the field to the gate at the far corner.

Below Ripon

It is possible to continue further downstream of the Ripon take-out all the way to the River Ouse. Approximately 3km further downstream, Boroughbridge Road (B6265) crosses the river. There is a very small rocky ledge directly downstream of the bridges, providing entertainment in the form of a small wave in certain conditions. Most powered craft going to Boroughbridge from Ripon follow Ripon Canal. The canal joins the Ure a couple of miles downstream of the B6265 bridge and all craft, powered or otherwise, share the river from this point. Other than the powered craft, the only other hazard worth mentioning is Westwick Locks and Weir just below Newby Hall, which should be portaged.

17 Lower Wharfe

 **OS Sheet 104** | **Bolton Abbey to Otley** | **22km**

Shuttle	A660 to the west, A65 to Addingham and the B6160 up to Bolton Bridge and Abbey (30 minutes).
Portages	At least two essential portages and two or three other weirs that require caution.
Start	△ Bolton Abbey, SE 079 550
Finish	○ Otley, SE 201 458

Introduction

Set in West Yorkshire's most beautiful National Park, the Wharfe offers gentle and scenic paddling with easy access to the river at several places. Higher up the Dale, the Wharfe offers good sport to whitewater paddlers who seek more challenging conditions, with Linton Falls and Appletreewick rapids being particular favourites. There is no reason why these should not be open-boated, but as they contain Grade 4 rapids they are often well described in other whitewater guide books. Just upstream from Bolton Abbey is The Strid, a well-known beauty spot, and a strange narrow chasm. The latter is very unsuitable for open canoes, but can be paddled in high water by kayaks and is well worth a visit to view it.

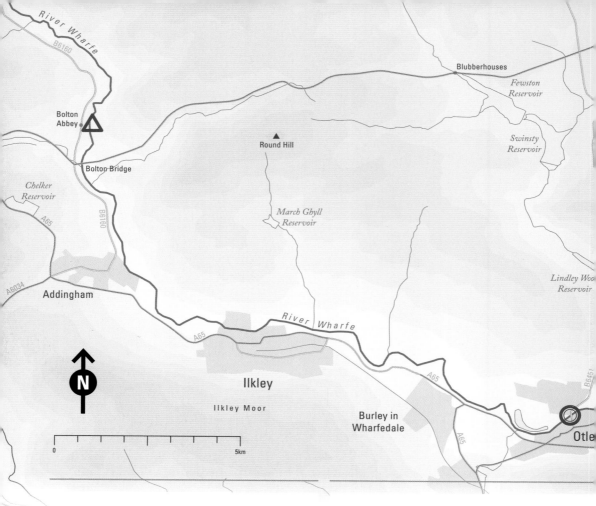

Water level

At Bolton Abbey, the small rapids should have enough water over them to paddle.

Campsites

A touring caravan site at Olicana Caravan Park, Addingham, open in the summer.

Access & egress

There are possible access or egress points at:

Old Bolton Bridge, SE 072 529

Lobwood Pumping Station
(emergency only), SE 075 519

Ilkley Lido, SE 122 484

Denton Bridge, Ilkley, SE 137 481.

This part of West Yorkshire is a popular destination for road cyclists and you are sure to meet some on the twisty rural lanes that snake around this part of the country. It is not a good place to be if you are in a hurry! Refreshment facilities take all forms here from tea rooms and country pubs to fine dining. Whatever your culinary requirements, you can find it here.

There are numerous places to access the river, as roads follow the river on both sides for much of its length. If you require a full day trip, Bolton Bridge to Otley should fit the bill nicely. Be warned however that, during the darker half of the year, the car park at Bolton Abbey declines entry from 4pm. If you would like a shorter and slightly more sedate journey, Ilkley to Otley offers a very pleasant alternative.

In addition to the marvellous Bolton Abbey, other local attractions include Middleton Woods located on the north of the Wharfe between Ilkley and Otley.

Although the river leaves its upper dale downstream of Bolton Abbey, the scenery remains pleasant and avoids the most urban parts of West Yorkshire.

Description

Paddlers getting on at Bolton can expect to pay to park their cars in the grounds of the historic Abbey. The beauty of the location, choice of launching spots and ease of access to the river will soon take any negative thoughts about payment and lock them firmly away. The river is playful here, with flowing but flat stretches punctuated with straightforward sections of Grade 2. Round a couple of bends and the Abbey comes into view, which is really quite special. Paddle under the footbridge (duck if the river is in flood) and on towards the village of Addingham. If you can't stomach paying for such easy and scenic access, the dead-end Beasley Lane opposite the Abbey Tearooms off the B6160 offers a place to unload boats for free at the Old Bolton Bridge via a footpath. Parking is very limited, however.

Before you reach the village of Addingham, Lobwood water pumping station appears on the right (west). A weir spans the river here, so caution is advised. Although long boats should pass through the tow back without incident, it looks very much like the recirculating water would hold a swimmer. Portage river right if you are in any doubt.

Still in the parish of Addingham, the river twists and turns then passes a caravan site (Olicana Caravan Park) on the right (west) bank. At the end of the caravan park is a sloping weir that guards the entrance to a section of river split by several small islands and littered with flood debris. Inspect before paddling, either by landing on one of the islands or scouting from the left bank. The river is gently flowing once past this, but once you have passed the church on the right and canoed under the suspension footbridge, be prepared to get out and walk around the first of two large stepped weirs between here and Otley.

Before you reach Ilkley, the river splits around a very large island. These are the second and third holes of Ilkley Golf Club, so it would seem like a good idea to stay in the wider main flow on the right-hand (south) side. To continue the sporting theme, Ilkley Tennis Club is also located on the right. The river turns sharp right then sharp left before arriving at Ilkley.

A clear view of a pretty 16th century stone bridge confirms arrival at Ilkley proper. Ilkley has four bridges that cross the river; the first is the nicest and the last, a suspension foot bridge, is the most significant to paddlers. Getting on and off the river at either of the two bridges that cross the river in the town centre is difficult and not advised, but access or egress is easy with ample parking at Ilkley Lido (the fourth bridge) at the outskirts of the town (SE 123 485).

After the lido the river passes through some stepping stones. These will need to be portaged in summer levels as there is an insufficient gap for a canoe to pass between them. Although the river follows the main road to Otley for much of its length, it is barely noticeable from the boat. The scenery is mostly agricultural with the occasional stone mill or house. There is a very large weir at Greenholme Farm about halfway between Ilkley and Otley, and it looks like it would make mincemeat of any boat that might try to descend it. Luckily the portage on river left is straightforward. There are stepping stones immediately downstream of the weir which may also need to be portaged at lower levels.

Although a mostly gentle affair, this section of the river does have the occasional easy rapid to keep one's interest.

The yacht masts of Otley Sailing Club appear on the left (north) bank and this indicates that the end of the trip is imminent. After a bend or two the bridge at Otley comes into view. Pass under the arches, dodging the bread being thrown to the ducks and swans that live there. Exit on the left bank via the steps and walk back towards the bridge through the small park to access the road. There is often kerbside parking here for loading but, failing that, the disused cattle market is opposite and plenty of space is available for loading there.

18 Leeds & Liverpool Canal

 OS Map 103 | **Kildwick to Gargrave** | **14km**

Shuttle	A629 and A65, 10km or 15 minutes.
Start	△ Kildwick village by swing bridge, SE 013 459
Finish	Gargrave, Holme Bridge, SD 934 545

Introduction

This is a lovely section of canal on the borders of Lancashire and Yorkshire, with views over much of the upper River Aire valley. Hills bound the northern side of this valley, with little hint of the built-up area north of this. Northwards is Malham Cove at the top of the Aire and upper Wharfedale. The Ribble valley is just to the west.

The jewel in the crown of this trip is the market town of Skipton ('sheep town'), a lovely traditional Yorkshire woollen town with old stone buildings, a market and a castle. Tourist narrow boats leave for trips on the Springs Branch from Belmont Wharf in the centre of the town, the former built to take stone out from quarries.

© Holme Bridge lock and sluice. L. and L. Canal

The start and finish of the trip is in small and quiet villages. Although this is not the summit stretch of the Leeds and Liverpool (which is very short), this route gives the paddler a peaceful and easy day out in an upper valley away from most of industrial Yorkshire.

The canal also lies on the main road route from Yorkshire to the Lake District, and is not far from the section of the River Ribble detailed in the Northwest section (Route 14). A paddler might also be tempted to explore the whole 127 miles of the canal, one of the longest in the UK.

Description

The canal is free of locks north from Keighley offering a longer paddle trip, but access and vehicle parking is more difficult. It is best to paddle this route first one way and then back or go as far as Skipton and back. Although the main road is always nearby, the canal (as with many others) remains a tranquil haven. Kildwick is a pretty village, and the start is on the east side of the road which crosses the canal on a swing bridge. A track leads into a parking area by the canal, and the paddler has to duck while canoeing under the bridge just after the start.

The White Lion pub is on the bank and the Parson's Bridge just after this has a part of a cemetery on either side. The River Aire on the left (west) side has an old packhorse bridge and Kildwick Hall, a 17th century manor house, is high on the hill on the right (east).

The village environs are quiet and, after just over a kilometre, the canal is alongside the

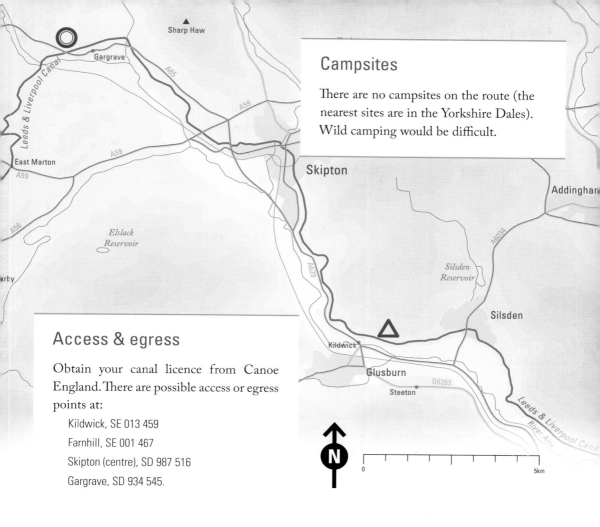

Campsites

There are no campsites on the route (the nearest sites are in the Yorkshire Dales). Wild camping would be difficult.

Access & egress

Obtain your canal licence from Canoe England. There are possible access or egress points at:

Kildwick, SE 013 459

Farnhill, SE 001 467

Skipton (centre), SD 987 516

Gargrave, SD 934 545.

main A629 road. Possible access can be obtained at Farnhill Bridge, which has a lay-by not far from the bridge. The 'Ings', the flat ground between the A629 and the River Aire, is an old Yorkshire name for flat ground that floods (the equivalent of the northeast or Scottish 'haughs').

Canal and road stay together until a swing out to the east takes the canal towards Low Bradley, another small village. After passing through another minor road swing bridge, the canal then turns back to the main road. The urban fringe of Skipton commences after 1km. The traffic noise subsides, and the 'stone canyon' through the centre is awe-inspiring. The canal basin is luckily in the centre of the town with vehicle parking nearby; this is a very pleasant place on a sunny day.

The main access is at the junction close to the impressive Skipton Castle of 1090 vintage where the Springs Branch (built to reach a limestone quarry) leaves to the east. The town is well worth a visit, as the castle is one of the best-preserved medieval castles in England. It was built by the Normans to keep the Scots at bay.

Springs Branch, Skipton L and L Canal

The canal then swings west as it leaves the town, the A629 crossing it on a concrete bridge before it joins the east–west A59. The railway is alongside the canal for a short time and the infant River Aire is also very close at one point. The Leeds and Liverpool then swings north to come alongside the A65, which heads northwest to Kirby Lonsdale and the Lake District. The scenery changes at this point from rather flat fields to more wooded areas. Gargrave beckons, the first of a number of small villages, as the road climbs northwest. Traffic is slow-moving through Gargrave. The first bridge, followed by a lock, is the end of the trip at Holme Bridge. Parking is available at the canal basin and quay for a short time to put boats on vehicles.

The village has all of the usual amenities and provides a pleasant and quiet end to an interesting day. This place on the canal is very nearly at the most northerly point of the whole canal length, before it turns and heads southwest through Lancashire.

19 River Ouse

 OS Sheet 99 | Linton-on-Ouse to York | 16km

Shuttle	A19 from York heading for Northallerton, turning off at Shipton for Newton-on-Ouse, Linton and Aldwark (35 minutes).
Portages	At a weir, Linton-on-Ouse.
Start	△ Linton-on-Ouse, SE 500 602
Finish	○ Marygate, York, SE 598 521

Introduction

The River Ouse flows through the beautiful Vale of York, one of England's most arable pieces of farmland located in a bowl between the Dales, the North Yorkshire Moors and the hilly East Riding. The start of the Ouse is downstream of the confluence of the Ure and Swale and just over two kilometres above the significant weir at Linton-on-Ouse. It flows through the City of York and was once a primary source of power and transport for the city. Tributaries of the Ouse include the Nidd, Wharfe, Aire, Don and Foss as well as the abovementioned Ure and Swale.

This trip can be lengthened as required, as it is possible to link this journey with either the Swale or Ure trips also described in the book (Routes 15 and 16). It is anticipated that travelling from Mickley Weir (Ure) to York would take around three days and from Catterick Bridge (Swale) to York around four days, depending on water levels, motivation and fitness! The Ouse can be paddled until it meets the Trent just short of the Humber Estuary, with the only obstacle being the weir and locks at Naburn some 6km south of York.

The City of York is indeed a fitting place to finish a canoe trip, one of England's most historic and picturesque cities with many attractions.

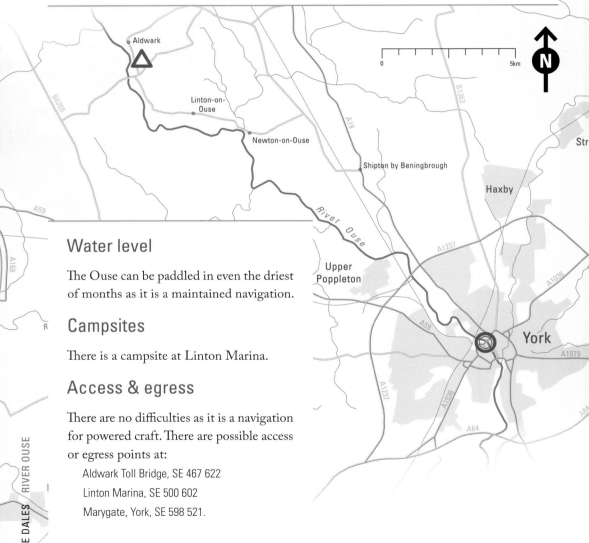

Water level

The Ouse can be paddled in even the driest of months as it is a maintained navigation.

Campsites

There is a campsite at Linton Marina.

Access & egress

There are no difficulties as it is a navigation for powered craft. There are possible access or egress points at:

Aldwark Toll Bridge, SE 467 622

Linton Marina, SE 500 602

Marygate, York, SE 598 521.

Description

Aldwark is about as far from York as one would wish to paddle in one day, approximately 22km. Getting on the river here is quite easy, although it may cost you money. The private toll bridge charges 40p for cars to cross the Ure here. On the upstream right (east) side is a picnic area where cars can be parked at no charge. The river is adjacent and only a grassy slope needs to be crossed to get to it. The disadvantage of getting on the river at Aldwark is that Linton Weir needs to be portaged 5km downstream. Do this via the right (south) bank to avoid having to pay a launch fee at the marina. If you choose to start your journey at Linton Marina this is pretty straightforward; just ensure that you access the water on the downstream side of the weir.

Linton is a massive weir; a canoe slalom was once planned to take place here using the fish ladders. The combination of one of the Ouse's famous floods (in summer) and the forecast weather conditions meant that the powers-that-be called the event off, never to be repeated.

Paddlers are greeted with a picturesque view of the village of Newton-on-Ouse almost straight after setting off from Linton-on-Ouse. Its church spire rises prominently from the flatness that is the Vale of York. Beningbrough Hall, a National Trust property, is passed on the left (east) bank another kilometre or so downstream. Although it is well screened by trees, brief glimpses of this grand Georgian house should be possible.

Aldwark toll bridge

Nun Monkton is situated on the outside of a sharp left-hand bend just over a kilometre downstream of Beningbrough Hall, and the River Nidd joins the Ouse here. The battle of Marston Moor, one of England's largest battles, was fought only a few miles away from Nun Monkton in 1664.

Beningbrough village on the left (east) consists mainly of farm buildings. The centre of York is about 11km from here. The river is quite straight with only gentle bends over the next few miles, and the village of Upper Poppleton coming into view on the right (west) will be a welcome sight for some.

After passing bridges carrying the railway line and York's ring road, you will notice the A19 and A59 running parallel on either side of the Ouse. Clifton Bridge comes into view after a final S-bend, signalling the home stretch if finishing in York. It is only a mile or so to Marygate now, and the river is often busy with tourist boats and people rowing. It might be worth carrying on to the infamous King's Arms pub between Ouse Bridge and Skeldergate Bridge. The pub is often featured in the news as it is regularly flooded.

York, founded in 71AD by the Romans and known as Eboracum, was occupied by Vikings and given the Scandinavian name of Jorvik. Its location of approximately halfway between London and Edinburgh was significant in the city's growth.

There are many places to take out in York but it is a busy tourist city, and street parking is controlled by permits and stringent timings. Marygate has a car park very close to the river and convenient steps for egress.

Greenholme stepping stones on the Wharfe

Soar at Thurmaston

Vale of Trent & East Midlands

We are now in the middle of England and the Trent, although not as large as either the Severn or Thames, is a major waterway. It is the third-longest river in England (260km) and a very important industrial artery. The river emerges from Trentham Gardens in the Potteries and flows southeast to Alrewas, northeast to Newark and then north to the Humber. For a river with a very industrial reputation, the upper reaches are pleasant and rural. Canals also follow the river valley all the way down.

We have included two different parts of the Trent in the book. The Penk joins the Trent at Stafford and the Sow joins at Great Haywood. One of the authors originally came from Wolverhampton, and the Penk, Sow and Trent journey was the first self-supported canoe camping trip undertaken in his teenage years. (This entailed a long walk into a muddy wood off the Shropshire Union Canal and three days of effort to get to Alrewas with a pal, where a phone call to a father with a car was not that well-received! However, such is the nature of intrepid expeditions.) Two beautiful small rivers of Derbyshire join the main river next; the Dove past Burton-on-Trent, still a major centre for brewing, and the Derwent at Derby.

The almost joined-up conurbation of Derby, Nottingham and Leicester alters the surroundings of the river but the Soar, another of our routes, flows in close to East Midlands airport in open countryside. Nottingham is skirted by the river, and Holme Pierrepont – the site of the National Watersports Centre and home to the first artificial canoe slalom course in the country and a 2km-long flat water sprint course – is located after Trent Bridge and the cricket ground.

The countryside is pleasant as far as Newark (a cathedral town) and also home to one of the first canoe slalom courses in England in the 1960s, although difficult to believe now. The river becomes tidal and canalised shortly after this, and is joined by the Fossdyke navigation from Lincoln, the Chesterfield canal after Gainsborough and the River Idle.

Near Scunthorpe the South Yorkshire Navigation leaves the Trent in a westerly direction heading for Sheffield, and at Trent Falls the Trent joins the Humber.

Trent at Great Haywood

20 Upper Trent

OS Sheet 27 | Stone to Great Haywood | 18.5km

Shuttle	A51, 30 minutes each way.
Portages	None (three locks if returning via the canal).
Start	△ Aston-by-Stone, SJ 907 326
Finish	◯ Great Haywood (or return up the Trent and Mersey Canal), SJ 995 225 or SJ 993 229

Introduction

The mighty River Trent has humble beginnings. In North Staffordshire, this tiny river leaves the famous Trentham Gardens near Stoke-on-Trent and winds its way past Stone, site of a famous and active canoe club. Relative to a great deal of industry further down, the Trent in these upper reaches is surprisingly rural and offers a relaxed journey through the pleasant pastureland of the Trent Valley.

The Trent and Mersey Canal follows the river closely along the stretch in this section, and runs from Long Eaton (near Derby) northwest to the Mersey at Preston Brook. Apart from being a cross-England waterway for trade, the canal was extremely important

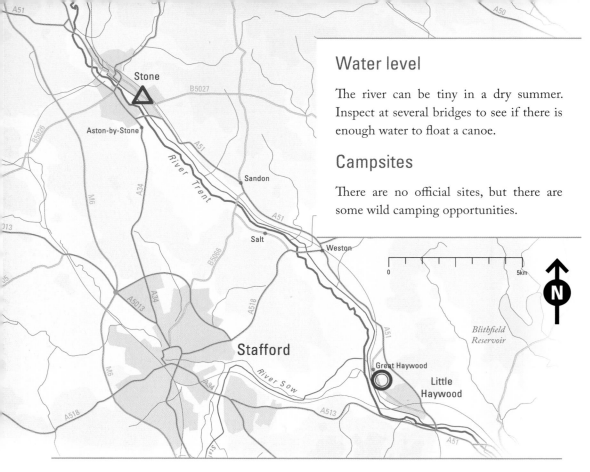

Water level

The river can be tiny in a dry summer. Inspect at several bridges to see if there is enough water to float a canoe.

Campsites

There are no official sites, but there are some wild camping opportunities.

in taking the products of the Potteries in North Staffordshire to the Mersey and the Manchester Ship Canal for export abroad to the rest of the British Empire.

The large stately home of Sandon Park is on the left (east) side when passing Salt. Weston Hall is on the right (west) bank and Shugborough Hall and Park are near Great Haywood at the end of the trip.

Access & egress

No access problems at all have been reported on this river. There are possible access or egress points at:

Aston-by-Stone, SJ 907 326

Salt, SJ 959 282

Great Haywood, SJ 995 225 or SJ 993 229.

To get to the start, take the A34 south from Stone towards Stafford. Look for a housing estate on the left and turn down Valley Road. A long grassy area and green fence indicate the presence of the river running parallel to the road. As the road bends, there is public access via a gate and a style. It is not a great place to park for extended periods, but it is quiet

Signpost at canal junction, Great Haywood

enough to park while sorting out kit and preparing for your journey. There is space for parking but it is a residential area, so take sensible precautions to keep your possessions safe.

Although the river is crossed at Sandon and also at Weston, getting access to the river from the road is tricky. A low bridge is however located between these at Salt. Although there is no signed public access there, it would not be difficult to move swiftly from the river to the road if required.

Great Haywood is the logical place to egress the Trent in these parts, and is a pretty place to leave the river. The most well-known egress point is the old and historic Essex or Packhorse Bridge, where both the canal and the Trent are crossed at this point. The Sow joins just before it, and the Trent has a small single drop here (the old ford). Access is very easy, although parking is a bit tricky. There is a teashop next to the lock at the bridge (the Trent and Mersey Canal runs parallel to the river here) with its own car park. There are not really any long-term parking solutions close to this egress point, but there is space to pause a vehicle while it is being loaded or unloaded.

An alternative is to egress some 500m before this bridge (SJ 995 230). There is both a road bridge and the Staffordshire and Worcestershire Canal aqueduct slightly higher up the Trent. Egress onto the left (east) bank and up the bank to the canal (a very well-worn trail). It is only 200m east on this canal to the junction with the Trent and Mersey Canal, passing the basin with many narrow boats, then left (north) up to the road bridge. Exit on to a car park for both a canal shop and tearoom.

109 VALE OF TRENT & EAST MIDLANDS UPPER TRENT

Description

This stretch seems to be paddleable most of the year. Even in summer months, the river keeps about 30cm of water in all but the driest of times. There are no significant hazards on the river other than bridges; only one bridge at Salt (which had debris on the upstream side of it at the time of writing and is relatively low) might require a measure of caution.

For the most part the river meanders gracefully through the gentle pasturelands of the Trent Valley. The banks are not especially high and the view can be taken in readily (depending on water level). Cows and horses will come to investigate the strange goings-on on the river. Other than the company of the grazing animals, you are unlikely to meet others on this trip. There are only a few footpaths that cross or follow the river at any point along this stretch. Although road noise can often be heard and trains occasionally spotted, this is a good paddle for those who enjoy solitude and peacefulness. Make sure you take all you will need for your journey as, until you arrive at Great Haywood, there is nowhere to get provisions once on the water.

Just before the Packhorse Bridge at Great Haywood, the river splits and what used to be an old fording place still exists. Depending on the water level, you may need to get out to help your boat over the rocky ledge that was once the ford. The River Sow joins from the right.

Egress is an easy and relaxed affair on either bank upstream of the bridge.

21 Penk, Sow & Trent

OS Sheet 127 | **Penkridge to Great Haywood** | **20km**

Shuttle	About 20 minutes via minor lanes.
Portages	Canal locks only (three near Penkridge) if using Staffordshire and Worcestershire Canal for return.
Start	△ Penkridge, Staffordshire, SJ 922 145
Finish	◎ Great Haywood (or Penkridge if circular route completed), SJ 995 225 or SJ 993 229

Introduction

This route introduces you to the lush countryside of South Staffordshire, the Penk having been a favourite of canoeists for many years. This trip can take the paddler down three rivers in one day. It leaves the pretty village of Penkridge, winds down to the environs of Stafford (the county town) and arrives on the Trent.

The Penk has been canoed in the past from the boundary of Wolverhampton, where the Shropshire Union Canal crosses the tiny river. It then winds north through Brewood, under the A5 and past Congreve before entering Penkridge. Unfortunately, the amount

© Penkridge

of water flowing nowadays is miniscule compared to that previously (an all-too-familiar situation).

This meandering journey through gentle arable farmland and Staffordshire suburbs can be broken down into several shorter sections or doubled in length and completed as a circular route by incorporating the Staffordshire and Worcestershire Canal. It would appear to be paddleable most of the year, but excessive vegetation both in the water and around the banks in summer months might hinder rapid progress. The village of Great Haywood is a picturesque finishing point or a convenient place to ready oneself for the return leg.

Access & egress

No access problems have been reported on these rivers. There are possible access or egress points at:

Penkridge Bridge, SJ 922 145

Tixal, SJ 975 215

Great Haywood, SJ 995 225 or SJ 993 229.

Getting on is very straightforward. The A449 on the north side of Penkridge crosses the River Penk. On the downstream side of the bridge on the right (south) is a very large car park belonging to a pub. There is easy access to the river from here and there seems to

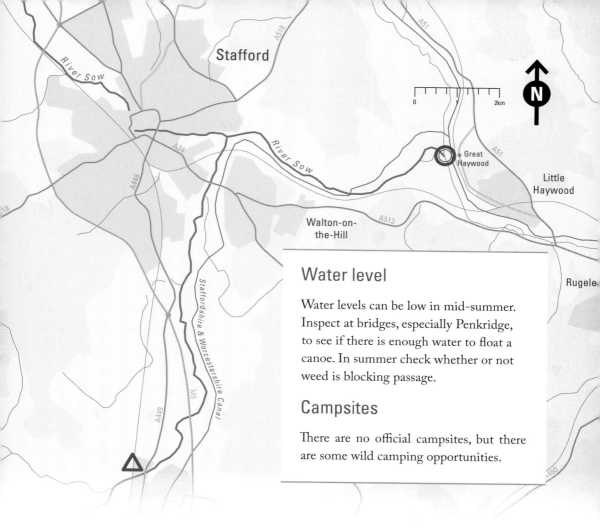

Water level

Water levels can be low in mid-summer. Inspect at bridges, especially Penkridge, to see if there is enough water to float a canoe. In summer check whether or not weed is blocking passage.

Campsites

There are no official campsites, but there are some wild camping opportunities.

be ample parking space. If you intend to return via the canal, you may wish to park your transport closer to the canal on the B5012.

There are several places you might consider getting off the river, but the most convenient by far is at Great Haywood. Here there is a beautiful historic old bridge known locally as the Packhorse or Essex Bridge. Both the canal and the Trent are crossed at this point and access is very easy, although parking is less so. Parking at the bridge is tight, although there is nearly always space to pull up for a drop and drive or a quick pick-up. The Lockhouse tearoom is right next to the canal, and has its own parking. It seems a nice place for a slice of civilisation. Longer-term parking is available in the village, but is much sought after. There is a pub almost next to the bridge with a large car park, but the landlord is not keen on paddlers using it (unless buying beer, one would assume).

An alternative at the end is to transfer onto the Trent and Mersey canal a few yards away and paddle 500m north past the junction with the Trent and Mersey Canal under the road bridge, to a large car park and canal shop and tearoom.

Description

It is fair to say that, if you seek thrills and excitement, this may not be the stretch of water for you. If however you are looking forward to a relaxed journey through pleasant countryside, punctuated by the occasional suggestion of civilisation, then give it a go.

While it is possible to join the River Penk at Cuttlestone Bridge, poor parking arrangements and significant bankside vegetation suggest that most will want to start their journey at Penkridge. Here the river is no more than 5m wide; its width barely alters until the confluence with the Sow some 12km downstream. A gentle flow even in summer levels is apparent and, provided the river weeds are not too dense, progress should be relaxed but steady. It is perhaps worth taking a pole along for this trip – paddles and vegetation are not always a happy marriage.

There are no footpaths along much of the river, but the Staffordshire and Worcestershire Canal is never very far away from it (meaning that a speedy U-turn is often possible). The B5012 separates the two for the first part of the trip, but after passing Acton Trussell the only thing that separates river and canal is fields. As the Penk bends and turns it often comes within metres of the canal, providing many opportunities to change experience. There are several places where roads cross the Penk, but getting access to the riverside is often difficult.

As you pass under the A513 road bridge on the outskirts of Stafford, watch out for the occasional shopping trolley; it is probably the only part of the river journey where such indignities may be experienced. You'll soon forget about them as the River Sow joins from the left (west) and adds a most welcome boost of volume and pace. From here you are paddling the Sow and, although the name has changed, it still runs parallel to the canal.

The scenery continues to be gentle and rambling, much like the River Sow itself. An aqueduct at Tixal gives an easy opportunity to switch from river to canal and start the journey back towards Penkridge if you wish, or carry on to Great Haywood on either waterway. The river has been split and diverted to flow past Shugborough Hall while the canal passes a swing bridge and another aqueduct near Haywood Mill. As the Staffordshire and Worcestershire Canal arrives at Great Haywood, it joins the Trent and Mersey Canal. The River Sow joins the River Trent and continues under that name until it meets the sea on the east coast near Hull.

Great Haywood seems an ideal place to end a one-way trip or a good place to pause before tackling the return journey. Egress from the river is simple from either bank upstream of the bridge (or see above for an alternative egress).

22 Middle Trent

 **OS Sheet 128** | **Willington to Castle Donington** | **13km**

Shuttle	A50 and A38, 11 miles or 15–20 minutes.
Grade	Grade 1, although Swarkestone rapid might be a little more in high water.
Start	△ Willington, Derbyshire, SK 296 279
Finish	○ Castle Donington, Derbyshire, SK 417 274

Introduction

This is a section of the River Trent that can be paddled all year. The Trent valley has highly varying scenery and is both industrial and agricultural, with large sand and gravel pits in the valley. This section of water lies between Burton-on-Trent upstream, famous for its several breweries in former times, and the large settlements of Long Eaton and Derby downstream. Along with many other English waterways, the Trent can be surprisingly rural in the midst of large towns or close to sizeable populations.

At Willington, the Trent is wide and gently flowing. It runs along the historic Swarkestone Causeway, passes through Derbyshire countryside and finishes where the counties of Nottinghamshire, Leicestershire and Derbyshire meet. The trip can be neatly split or shortened via the bridge at Swarkestone, where access is also very easy.

Water level

The river is always canoeable, but care should be taken in flood conditions as the Trent becomes large and fast.

Campsites

There are few official sites, although there are some wild camping opportunities. There is a formal campsite at Shardlow Marina some 6km downstream from the finish.

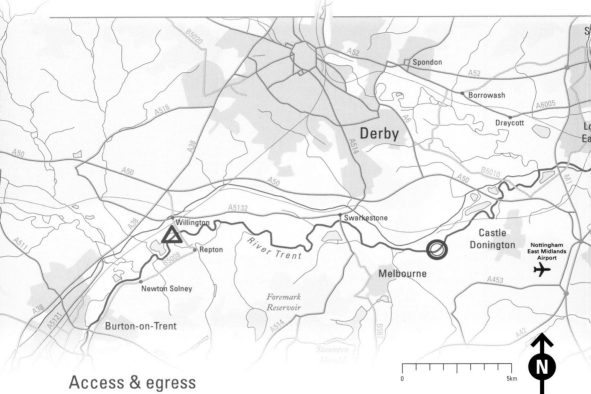

Access & egress

There are possible access or egress points at:

Willington, SK 296 279

Swarkestone, SK 369 285

The Priest House, Castle Donington, SK 417 274.

The road bridge that crosses the Trent at Willington is an ideal place to launch from. A public path on the upstream side of the bridge on the Willington side has a straightforward path to a grassy bank on which to prepare for the journey ahead. Parking near the bridge is not easy but, at the time of writing, there were opportunities to park in front of several disused buildings very close to the bridge.

There is a large, gated car park at the Priest House Hotel at Castle Donington. The hotel has a long history of welcoming canoeists and continues to do so. All the hotel asks for is a fee for using its facilities, although this will often be waived if those concerned spend a

Trent at Willington

little time in the bar for cup of tea or perhaps something stronger. The hotel suggests that those wishing to gain access to the river in their grounds check that there is not a private function on, as the grounds would be closed to the public on those occasions.

If you wish a shorter trip, Swarkestone Bridge can be used to access or egress the river. There is ample parking on the right (south) side of the river, just off the road to Ingleby.

Description

The Trent is a wide and significant river at Willington and measures perhaps 40–50m from shore to shore. The current flows gently but perceptibly and the bridge piers make distinct eddy lines.

Don't let the vista of the power station in the distance put you off; the river flows through farmland here and, once out of the shadow of Willington, the scene is very rural for the remainder of the journey. The river has some large bends in it and has created new paths in one or two places, giving paddlers a choice of routes (none of which are wrong). The river moves at a constant pace around the large sweeping bends, giving paddlers ample opportunities to practise their skills free of the risk of obstructions.

At Swarkestone Bridge, part of the longest stone bridge (Swarkestone Causeway) in England, the river has some pace to it and jets and eddies are created by the bridge structure. A small drop occurs in a line across the river just downstream of the bridge. This can be a great place to pause and refresh those moving water skills or stop and stretch the legs, as access to the bank is easy. This was, surprisingly, the site of an annual slalom competition many years ago, with camping on the right (south) bank next to the road. A pub on the left (north) might provide a lunch for those who have not brought sufficient provisions. The rural feel to Swarkestone means it is easy to forget that the city of Derby lies just to the north.

Swarkestone Bridge

Locals would have you believe that the 13th century causeway was built as a result of two sisters witnessing their lovers drown while trying to cross the Trent flood-plain in high water. The sisters saw their men swept away by the river. Traumatised by this, they vowed that no-one else would suffer the same fate. They devoted the rest of their lives to building the causeway and its bridge, leaving them penniless when they died.

The river narrows and picks up a little as you approach the Priest House at Castle Donington. Locals often use this location for introducing novice paddlers to moving water skills, and there are no significant hazards other than a fairly sharp left-hand bend. Here, you are surrounded by human activity. The famous Castle Donington Raceway (used mainly for motor-cycle racing) is just on the right up the hill, and East Midlands Airport lies ahead. The hotel is very obvious and egress is on river right.

Downstream from here the Trent really does become a much more canalised and industrial river with some very large gravel lagoons from old workings. It soon enters Nottingham City suburbs and passes both the Trent Bridge Cricket Ground and (perhaps of more interest to canoeists) the Holme Pierrepoint whitewater course, where all of the UK's aspiring canoeing athletes have to train.

Paddlers at Leicester

23 Soar

OS Sheet 129 | **Leicester to Trent Confluence** | **37km**

Shuttle	A6 from Leicester Outdoor Pursuits Centre (LOPC) to Barrow upon Soar (20 minutes). A6, A50 and minor roads from LOPC to Trent confluence (35 minutes).
Portages	Many locks; some must be portaged but some have weirs that can be shot with care.
Start	△ LOPC, Leicester, SK 591 076
Finish	○ Barrow upon Soar marina and caravan park, SK 585 166 (16km) or Trent confluence, SK 490 311 (37km)

Introduction

The River Soar is the major waterway of Leicestershire. From its source near Hinckley, it runs in a north-westerly direction towards Leicester and then almost due north, passing Loughborough on its way to the River Trent at Trent Locks. From Leicester the Soar forms part of the Grand Union Canal and there are 21 locks on its 28 navigable miles between the city and the river's confluence with the Trent. Although some of the locks have shootable weirs, many of them require portaging. With the exception of Leicester

© Zouch Weir

and Loughborough, the river runs mostly through agricultural land. There are open arable plains to the east and the uplands of Charnwood Forest to the west.

The Soar was once an important resource for the city of Leicester's thriving hosiery industry. Many factories used the water in one way or another to produce knitted garments; it was also critical in providing a source of power as well as the means to transport the finished goods. Although the Soar is now regarded as a relatively clean river, pollution caused by the washing and dying of textile goods was once a real problem and resulted in the river becoming a fetching shade of pink. Wildlife now thrives on the river and, despite being navigable, paddlers will often find themselves quite alone with the exception of swans or other aquatic birds.

The waste produced by the Industrial Revolution of the 18th century was not the only thing to pollute the Soar. It is recorded that after the Battle of Bosworth in the 15th century the body of Richard III was treated very badly by Henry Tudor. Ten years later, Henry VII had the remains placed in a tomb at Greyfriars Church where they remained until the Dissolution of the Monasteries. The tombs were smashed, the skeleton was thrown into the River Soar and the sarcophagus used as a horse trough.

A simple journey following the path of the Grand Union Canal is possible all year around, although care should be taken after heavy rainfall. There is also a possible circular route that uses the original course of the Soar and loops through Loughborough on the man-made canal.

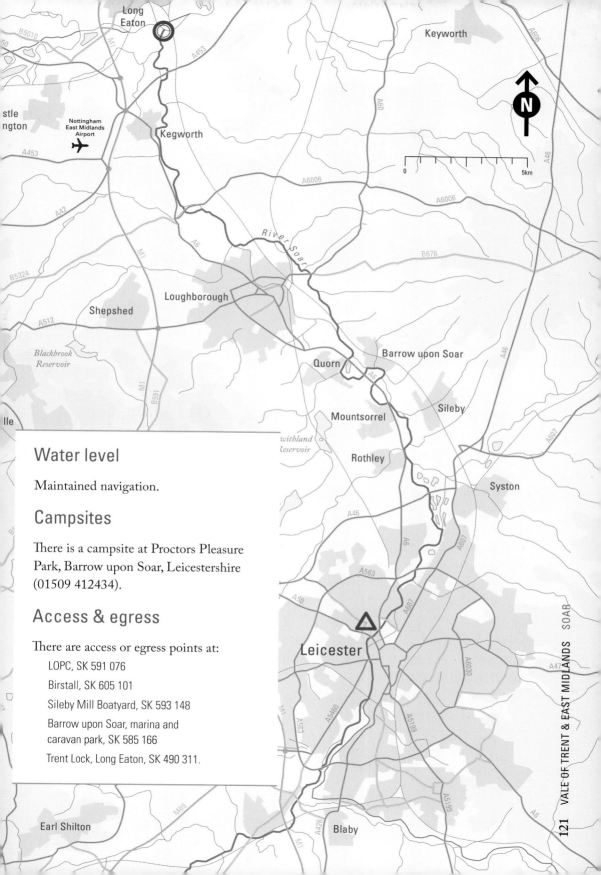

Water level

Maintained navigation.

Campsites

There is a campsite at Proctors Pleasure Park, Barrow upon Soar, Leicestershire (01509 412434).

Access & egress

There are access or egress points at:

LOPC, SK 591 076

Birstall, SK 605 101

Sileby Mill Boatyard, SK 593 148

Barrow upon Soar, marina and caravan park, SK 585 166

Trent Lock, Long Eaton, SK 490 311.

Description

The easiest place to put in is at Leicester Outdoor Pursuits Centre. It is possible to put in further upstream, but the ease of parking and access to the river make starting here an obvious choice. The centre has long been used to introduce people young and old to the pleasures of paddling. One of the authors first learned to kayak here while in the Scouts, and returned in adulthood to work on summer programs for local school children.

The river here is very gently flowing but you soon make progress downstream. Thoughts of having to rush have drifted away within a few bends and the cruising begins. Birstall Lock comes into view after 4km. There is a mill stream on the left (west) with a 1.5m weir, but walking around the lock is the recommended action (and is advised at nearly all of the locks on the Soar).

Thurmaston Mill Lock is the next portage a further 4km on. There is a marina here and several useful shops in the village. Paddle on and resist the temptation to investigate the original path of the Soar as it leaves the canal off to the left (west). Heavy vegetation, weeds and a weir await those who are tempted to venture away from the order of the Grand Union Canal. Those with a thirst will be pleased to see the Hope and Anchor pub coming into view as they pass Wanlip Reservoir 3.5km further on. The River Wreak joins from the right (east) and then Junction Lock must be negotiated. The Soar returns from the left and almost immediately you arrive at Cossington Lock which has a weir off to the right.

Sileby Mill and Lock are located 3.5km on from Cossington. There is a weir on the right (east); inspect carefully before paddling if you intend to run the not-insignificant feature. The original course of the river leaves to the right over a weir; the main advantage of choosing to follow this lesser waterway is that it bypasses the lock after Cossington. Those seeking a reliable water level should however stay on the navigation. Mountsorrel Lock has a public house by the water: the Swan Inn. It is quite possible that refreshment might be needed here as the portage (on the right) is not the easiest. While the weir on the left might be considered paddleable by some, it will be a far from pleasant prospect for those who value their boats.

Shortly after the Soar rejoins the navigation, the village of Barrow upon Soar comes into view and the paddler will soon be presented with an interesting decision to make. The river splits off to the left (west) and past the hamlet of Quorn. This detour adds 4km to distance travelled compared to simply following the navigation on the right. There is a lock at Barrow to portage, and the village has a campsite and the usual local amenities.

It's not often you come across a dinosaur when paddling, but if interested Barrow upon Soar would be a good place to look. A Plesiosaur fossil was found in Barrow upon Soar in 1851, hence the village emblem. This prehistoric marine reptile lived approximately 175 million years ago and was common in Leicestershire. Copies of the fossil, referred to as 'The Kipper' by locals, can be seen on the traffic island in Barrow.

Paddlers have another decision to make about 2km downstream from Barrow. At Pillings Lock you can go left (west) and follow the navigation through the University town of Loughborough, or go right past the weir and paddle along the original course of the river. The two meet up again after about 13km, so a circular route is possible. The navigation offers the reliability of a consistent water level, while the river offers superior vistas.

If following the river, the water passes over a weir at Coates Mill on the outskirts of Loughborough. This is a very popular spot for those who prefer fishing to boating and it can get very busy here. The river is often shallow on ths section and not well suited to kayaks. Canoes may only float along much of this stretch, but may benefit from being unoccupied at times. If in doubt, stay on the navigation.

The river now flows gently through arable farmland and past the villages of Stanford on Soar, Normanton on Soar, Zouch and Kegworth until it reaches the Trent. The distance from Barrow to the Trent confluence is about 22.5km and has only 8 locks to portage or paddle around.

Egress can be made easily on the north bank of the Trent. There is ample car parking there and the Trent Navigation pub for some refreshment.

Wheaton Ashton, Shropshire Union Canal

West Midlands

This area includes the west side of Staffordshire, the south of Shropshire and the north of Worcestershire. Although the countryside is very rural and unspoilt, it is not valued very highly by the casual visitor. It includes some of the prettiest villages and scenery in England however, although (as with many British regions) large industrial towns are not far away.

As well as the central area of the Black Country (so-called because the place was very black from industrial smokestacks until the 1950s), Shropshire hides an area unknown to many visitors until they become tourists and read the local literature. The remains of a very old coal and iron industry lie in the Ironbridge Gorge, now hidden by small wooded hills (a great place to explore).

The valley of the Severn totally dominates the landscape, one of England's truly great rivers. The river winds its way from the flat plains of north Shropshire to Shrewsbury, a masterpiece of a medieval fortified hill town from where the Welsh could be shot (legally) by bowmen. It then follows the Ironbridge Gorge area and pastoral countryside down through Bridgnorth to Bewdley, two beautiful little towns. The straight line of the Shropshire Union Canal crosses the landscape from Staffordshire to Shropshire, and into Cheshire.

The section on the valley of the Trent (Route 20) is not set very far from the two waterways in this section, and travel from one part to another is straightforward. The only difference is in the watersheds: the Trent flows into the Humber and the North Sea and the Severn flows southwest into the Bristol Channel.

Most of the Severn in England has been included (Route 24), as this is both an easy river (ideal for canoe-camping) and navigation with enough variety to satisfy all paddlers.

24 Severn

OS Sheets 126, 127, & 138 | **Pool Quay to Bewdley** | **130km (3–4 days)**

Shuttle	West along the A456 and A4117 to Ludlow, the A49 to Craven Arms and then the A489 and A490 northwest to Welshpool which is only a few miles south of Pool Quay (54 miles, 90 minutes).
Grade	1–2; Jackfield rapid near Ironbridge is possibly harder than Grade 2 in high water.
Portages	Shrewsbury Weir
Start	△ Pool Quay, SJ 258 115
Finish	◎ Bewdley, SO 789 751

Introduction

The Severn can be done from mid-Wales at about Newtown, 30km higher up. The authors have never encountered much water up here, but don't let us put you off! The reason for suggesting Pool Quay is that the Severn Navigation begins here.

The trip described finishes at Bewdley. If you have the time, you can also paddle the 75km down to Gloucester. After Bewdley there are compulsory portages around weirs, and

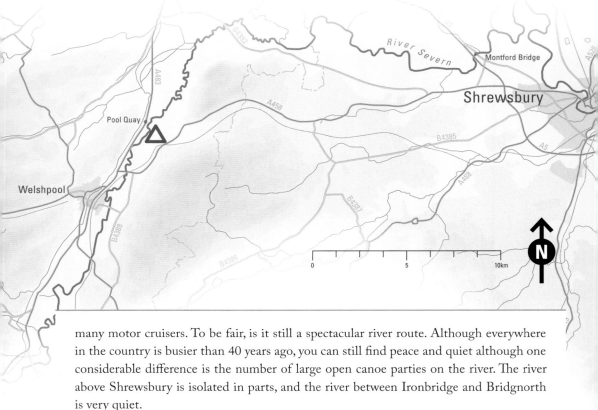

many motor cruisers. To be fair, is it still a spectacular river route. Although everywhere in the country is busier than 40 years ago, you can still find peace and quiet although one considerable difference is the number of large open canoe parties on the river. The river above Shrewsbury is isolated in parts, and the river between Ironbridge and Bridgnorth is very quiet.

Many English people have never travelled to old, industrial Shropshire. The old and quaint towns of the Ironbridge Gorge are well worth visiting however, and are now classified as a UNESCO World Heritage site. Be a tourist and enjoy the sights.

Severn memories

The Severn has to be one of the classics: a long navigation with very varied scenery and nearly always enough water flow. It is one of my personal favourites, being the first 'proper' river I ever paddled on. My first trip undertaken with Wolverhampton Canoe Club (apart from on local ditches and canals) was the Severn from Bridgnorth to Bewdley, possibly the prettiest and most popular day trip. I was lucky enough to live only 13 miles from the river, so it became important in my youth. It provided my first-ever canoe-camping trip, the first rapids ever paddled (at Jackfield and Eymore) and the first river I ever paddled from beginning to the end. My memories are of sliding peacefully down the river between sandstone cliffs, silent green tunnels of trees and delightful old pubs.   Eddie

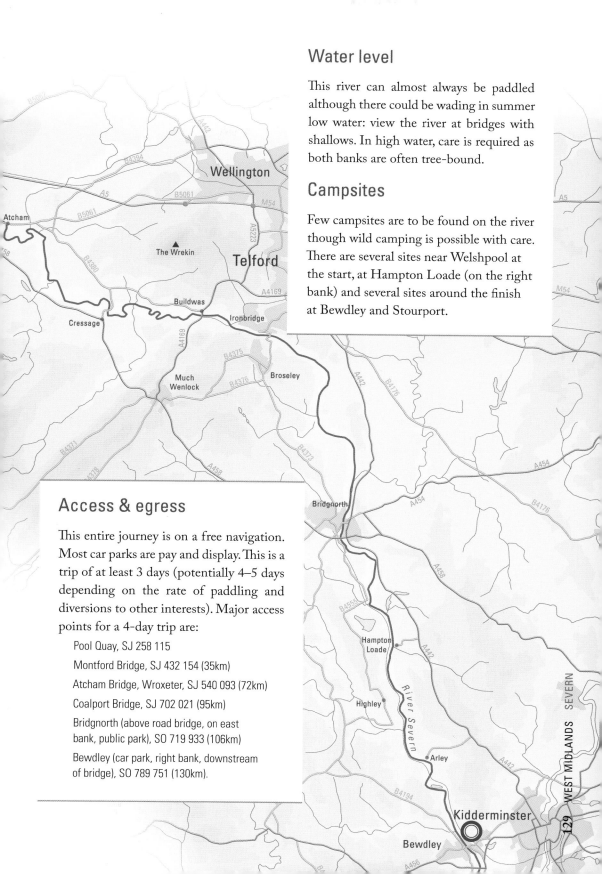

Water level

This river can almost always be paddled although there could be wading in summer low water: view the river at bridges with shallows. In high water, care is required as both banks are often tree-bound.

Campsites

Few campsites are to be found on the river though wild camping is possible with care. There are several sites near Welshpool at the start, at Hampton Loade (on the right bank) and several sites around the finish at Bewdley and Stourport.

Access & egress

This entire journey is on a free navigation. Most car parks are pay and display. This is a trip of at least 3 days (potentially 4–5 days depending on the rate of paddling and diversions to other interests). Major access points for a 4-day trip are:

Pool Quay, SJ 258 115

Montford Bridge, SJ 432 154 (35km)

Atcham Bridge, Wroxeter, SJ 540 093 (72km)

Coalport Bridge, SJ 702 021 (95km)

Bridgnorth (above road bridge, on east bank, public park), SO 719 933 (106km)

Bewdley (car park, right bank, downstream of bridge), SO 789 751 (130km).

Description

This part of the river commencing at Pool Quay (9–10km from England) is in the countryside where it is obvious that the hills of Wales are giving way to a flatter and more agricultural landscape. Ahead are the bumpy small hills of Moel y Golfa, Breidden and Middletown, around which the Severn winds. The Severn Way footpath will be following you all the way down, taking a shortcut across some of the large river loops.

Llandrinio Bridge (with little parking) is at 12.5km and the River Vyrnwy (a spectacular whitewater river in its upper reaches) joins from the left (north) just before Crewgreen village and bridge. The river then meanders over a flat plain towards Shrewsbury. The Royal hill, pub and campsite are left (north) at 22km. Shrawardine village is on the left bank after about another 6km, and a motte-and-bailey castle is located the right bank.

Montford Bridge at 35km heralds Shrewsbury to those driving down the A5 from Wales, but there is still a long way to go by river. The village is followed by the very long (6km) loop, nearly an oxbow, of Isle Grange. There is a possible portage along a farm lane if you want to cut the corner, but please ask permission if encountering anybody from the farm.

Shrewsbury is one of England's gems, a lovely red brick town on an obvious defensive hill with an easily defended large bend in the river. It is a prosperous market town but also a commuter hideaway within daily reach of the industrial West Midlands. The town is worth a short visit and provides a useful lunch stop on the journey (there is a portage on the weir anyway).

Welsh Bridge is reached after 53km, English Bridge after 55km and then a railway bridge; the weir is just downstream. It can be portaged by taking out on the grassy right bank before it. This is followed by four more road crossings and another railway bridge before you leave the town behind.

The next village is Atcham at 68km, and hills start appearing in the distance ahead. Wroxeter, 4km after Atcham, is a very important Roman city site and is one of many scattered along the route of the old A5 road (Watling Street).

The river now starts to speed up perceptibly, and at Cressage Bridge (80km) the river enters a noticeably narrower and wooded valley. The village of Buildwas is heralded for miles ahead by the very obvious power station cooling towers (88km). After many miles of little to see, bridges abound with Buildwas road bridge (the A4169 Much Wenlock to Telford road), a minor road bridge, the railway bridge into the power station for coal trains and, after another 1km, the famous and instantly recognisable Iron Bridge of Telford. As a paddler, you can see the structure easily from underneath. If spending a night in this area, the various industrial heritage attractions are well worth viewing.

Shropshire's industrial past

The Ironbridge Gorge Museums (http://www.ironbridge.org.uk/) are scattered over ten different sites; any worthwhile visit is going to take the tourist more than a day. Among these tiny villages, hills and woods, men taught themselves to forge iron on an industrial scale. They used it for many industrial and household purposes and developed the canals, railways and the Victorian-Age-style of living. Visit Blists Hill Victorian Town, Enginuity, Coalbrookdale Museum of Iron, Darby Houses, Jackfield Tile Museum, Coalport China Museum, Museum of the Gorge, the Iron Bridge and Tollhouse, Broseley Pipeworks and the Tar Tunnel.

Shortly after Ironbridge is a new road bridge, followed by the largest rapid on the river which was formed in the late 20th century by road construction rubble. It is one wave on a very narrow section and unavoidable. If wanting to view this, land well upstream. The effect of this 'artificial' rapid has been to denude the former Jackfield rapid (1km downstream) of both any height of water and power; this was a slalom course in former times. The former pub on the right (northeast) bank is now derelict and a sad sight. Coalport follows (95km) with a bridge, and then the river enters a long wooded stretch for the 11km down to Bridgnorth.

The scenery totally changes from this point: the vague and coaly remains of the Ironbridge area are replaced by lush pasture and woodland. The banks reveal very little apart from signs of the Apley Park estate on the left (east) bank. Eventually the river widens, the tiny River Worfe enters from the left in a marshy area and red sandstone cliffs on the left side herald the A442 road joining the left bank.

Bridgnorth is near (106km) when a golf course is seen on the right (west) bank. The church towers of the High Town are soon seen on the right, emerging rather suddenly from the wooded river. The good access point is on the left (east) in a public park before the old road bridge. Bridgnorth is a beautiful old town for its many old black-and-white Tudor buildings. The Low Town is at river level, and used to flood regularly. The High Town contains most of the shops and the market place. A funicular railway can carry you up to the High Town.

One of the best day canoe trips in the country then follows. The 24km down to Bewdley is punctuated by lovely small villages and the presence of the Severn Valley Railway; the steam trains are always seen and heard on summer weekends. After Bridgnorth slips away, the new road by-pass bridge is overhead and the village of Quatford is high on the left (east) bank. Hampton Loade 9km downstream is a popular stop, mainly for the Lion pub on the left bank. A rope ferry runs over the river and there is a campsite on the right (west) bank which is very busy in summer. The river sweeps lazily around large bends with many trees and shallows.

The former mining village of Highley follows after a further 4km; although the village is hardly visible the pub can be seen high on the right bank. The village of Arley (Upper Arley on the map) after another 4km has a very useful shop and a pub. The ferry ramps from the 1950s–60s car ferry are clearly visible (now used by canoeists), and a recent metal footbridge crosses the river after the village. Arley is flooded by day trippers in the summer, and there are many caravans and huts in the area. Robert Plant of rock music fame (Led Zeppelin) has a house in the woodland near Arley, betraying his original midland roots.

The Severn has one piece of excitement left in the final 7km down to Bewdley: Eymore rapid. It is worth paying attention if paddling a loaded open canoe in high water. A railway bridge (for the Severn Valley Railway) crosses shortly below Arley. An island is encountered after a long bend to the left, and the left side should be taken while keeping close to the island. The river picks up speed and there is a small fall visible on the left side; an obvious 'V' indicates the route on the right. The river bends sharply to the right just after this.

From here to Bewdley is a bit of a slog on flat water. A pipe bridge is passed under after Eymore and a former railway bridge at Dowles heralds your arrival at Bewdley. This last kilometre is frequently used by the local rowing club. The main road bridge signals the end of the journey at a car park on the right (west) side after the bridge, where the wall gives way to a grassy bank. There is no other easy exit off the river. Stay awhile in Bewdley, another lovely little town with Georgian, Victorian and Edwardian buildings.

An alternative trip if you are short of time and can't do the whole of the stretch described is to paddle the section from Bridgnorth to Bewdley (23km).

25 Shropshire Union Canal

OS Sheet 127 | **Wolverhampton to Market Drayton** | **52.5km (or 40km)**

Shuttle	A529 and A41 from Market Drayton (32 miles, 1 hour).
Portages	None on the shorter route (two locks on the longer route).
Start	△ Autherley Junction (with the Staffordshire and Worcestershire Canal), Wolverhampton, SJ 901 020 or Wheaton Aston, Shropshire, SJ 858 127
Finish	○ Tyrley locks near Market Drayton, Shropshire, SJ 690 324

Introduction

The Shropshire Union is one of the most pleasant of English canals, taking the navigator from the heart of the industrial Midlands into the quiet of the Shropshire countryside and on to Chester and the River Dee. Ironically, most of the canal winds through Staffordshire and Cheshire and not Shropshire.

This canal was built to link Wolverhampton, sitting at the northwest end of the Black Country, with the Manchester Ship Canal at Ellesmere Port so that the many manufactured goods produced in the Midlands could reach an export port. It was one of the last major canals to be built in England and is not a 'contour canal' (which follows the lie of

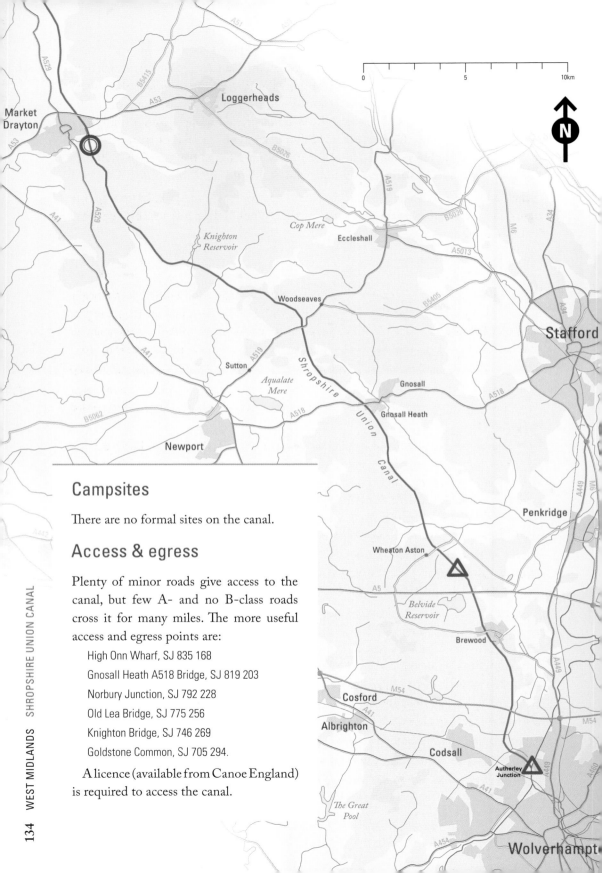

0   5   10km

N

Campsites

There are no formal sites on the canal.

Access & egress

Plenty of minor roads give access to the canal, but few A- and no B-class roads cross it for many miles. The more useful access and egress points are:

High Onn Wharf, SJ 835 168

Gnosall Heath A518 Bridge, SJ 819 203

Norbury Junction, SJ 792 228

Old Lea Bridge, SJ 775 256

Knighton Bridge, SJ 746 269

Goldstone Common, SJ 705 294.

A licence (available from Canoe England) is required to access the canal.

the land) but is almost a straight line across the countryside. An embankment was built with much difficulty due to slippage near Norbury Junction, where the former Shrewsbury Canal left to the west. Its construction was forced by an uncooperative landowner who did not want the canal crossing his land. Even although the 'Shroppie' crosses Shropshire in almost a straight line, this does not make it uninteresting. The lovely Llangollen Canal leaves to the west at Hurleston Junction just after Nantwich, and the Middlewich Branch heads east soon after at Barbridge Junction with the Trent and Mersey Canal.

The canal is so pretty and unspoilt that it has been proposed for World Heritage Site status, and you will meet many pleasure craft here. Wildlife, especially water birds, thrive on this waterway.

Description

We are giving the paddler a choice in this route: either a long paddle with no locks (beginning at Wheaton Aston) or an even longer trip with just one lock portage (beginning at Autherley Junction). Leaving from Wolverhampton, you wind out of the city into unspoilt countryside. The trip can be shortened by using one of the other available access points.

Autherley Junction (not to be confused with Aldersley Junction, just south of here) is fairly rural but was once an important terminus; until the 1960s it possessed large warehouses. There is a shop here now for the many boaters and the local boat club is based in old stables.

On leaving the junction the paddler is between fields with the Barnhurst Sewage Works on the left (west). The Pendeford estate on the right was built on the former Wolverhampton airfield, which once featured in a Jack Hawkins thriller film. The main road bridge linking northern Wolverhampton with the pretty commuter village of Codsall comes after the Pendeford road bridge and Wolverhampton boat club. The tiny River Penk passes under the canal (featured in Route 21), the upper section of which was paddled by one of the authors many years ago. In soft-skinned kayaks, a teenage canoe-camping adventure party made its way through many woods. The first 11km or so took a whole day, which was mainly spent walking or wading!

The M54 road bridge heralds a wooded section with the Avenue Bridge carrying an estate road west to Chillingham Hall, home of the locally famous Gifford family. Brewood (pronounced 'Brood') village follows, a pretty and ancient Staffordshire village. This area had many connections with Charles II; Boscobel House lies about three miles to the west where he is both reputed to have hidden in an oak tree from Cromwell (now the Royal Oak, precursor to many a pub name) and used one of the several 'priest holes' in the house, which were used to hide Catholic priests from the Roundheads. Boscobel is one of the best examples of such a house left in England.

The canal crosses the A5 at the Watling Street on Telford's Stretton aqueduct, a fine example of cast-iron trough and railings. Lapley Wood Cutting, where there is a rock in the water painted to look like a crocodile, follows after a slight turn to the left. The two Wheaton Aston locks (the alternative starting point) are soon reached (12km), with road access via a pub car park on the left (west) bank after the locks. The moorings are very busy here, with many narrow boats.

There now follows a 27km 'pound' (a stretch without locks), the longest on the Shroppie. A former WW2 airfield can be seen on the left (west) after 2km, followed by a hall with moat before the village of Little Onn with its own wharf. Woods and hedges abound on this stretch and soon the short Cowley tunnel is reached, now some 70m instead of an original 600m after a series of collapses. The canal is now in a long cutting as a result, spectacularly covered with ivy, moss and lichens.

The A518 crosses at Gnosall Heath, followed by a disused railway bridge. Shelmore Wood is soon after, the site of the re-aligning of the canal line on an embankment built mainly of marl (clay) to the west of the original line (18m high and 1.6km long). The Shropshire countryside to the west is becoming flatter now and there are views of Aqualate Mere, one of the first of the Shropshire meres to be glimpsed. The Wrekin, a famous and popular Shropshire hill, is about 400m high.

A 200m-long canal basin, all that remains of the branch to Newport (originally planned to run to Shrewsbury), can be seen at Norbury Junction (24km). There is easy access to the A519 via a narrow village road. The basin has parking and many narrow boats. It is easy to imagine what this place was like 200 years ago, with agricultural produce being shipped out and household supplies coming in.

The A519 crosses on a very high bridge with a telegraph pole halfway up it, followed by Grub Cutting (1.6km long). High Offley has a pub on the bank and Shebdon Great Bank follows. The countryside around here is very quiet, with little traffic.

Knighton is the next village (32km from Autherley, 20km from Wheaton Aston), the former site of a Cadbury's chocolate factory which received milk from the surrounding areas by canal. The canal passes into Shropshire from Staffordshire soon after, only to enter Cheshire a few miles later.

The countryside opens out around Little Soudley with great views, before the Woodseaves Cutting blocks out the light. The 2.4km-long stretch is very damp and cold, although the flora is worth the discomfort.

The paddler is now reaching the end of the journey as the first of the Tyrley Locks appears. The canoeist will want to portage the five locks, road access being from the bridge at the higher end of the locks. Although parking is limited, access is usually possible (except perhaps on a summer weekend). Tyrley is very quiet for most of the time, the nearest habitation being Market Drayton two miles away.

GRAND UNION CANAL CARRYING CO LTD
REGISTERED AT BRENTFORD Nº 603
PHONE ROYAL 5630
PORT of LONDON BUILDING E.C.3
RIGAL
G.U 12500
364

Ⓒ Wheaton Ashton, Shropshire Union Canal

Index

Venture Canoes®

Explore the water

Prospector

MANUFACTURED IN GREAT BRITAIN